Albert Bright

AstronSpaceOnomy Solutions

The Formulas of Astronomy as Solutions for Liberty and Peace

© 2019 Albert Bright
      1st German edition: 2019
© 2021 Albert Bright
      1st British edition – as 2/3 trilogy of GlobalOnomy, 2021

ISBN Paperback: 9783753445472

9 783753 445472

Publisher: www.world-wide-wealth.com

Author: Albert Bright

Envelope design, illustration: Albert Bright,

Editor, proofreading: www.world-wide-wealth.com,

Translation: www.world-wide-wealth.com

Publisher & Print: BoD, Books on Demand GmbH, Norderstedt / Hamburg, Germany

VG-WORT (German Patent Office) monitored content usage.

Bibliographic information of the German National Library:

The German National Library records this publication in the German National Bibliography; detailed bibliographic data can be found on the Internet via http://dnb.dnb.de .

This book arose from the fascination of the universe with its seemingly limitless dimensions and growth - and the idea of using its laws of nature as a recipe for a better world.

Albert Bright

The laws of astronomy to overcome challenges from economy & currency, knowledge & wisdom, liberty & peace, health & wealth, as well as welfare & sustainability - world-wide!

Table

A. INTRODUCTION, 1

B. SPACE: DIMENSIONS & VALUE IDEAS, 4

B.1. General aspects of space, 4

B.2. General Earth aspects of space, 9

B.3. General Universe aspects of space, 18

B.4. General relativity aspects of space, 26

B.5. Other astronomical aspects of space, 35

B.6. The space formula, 55

B.7. Justification of speed approach for "c² ", 62

B.8. (Cross) correlations – as SPACE formula justification, 71

C. Spatial Aspects in economic models - and sociological dimensions, 92

C.1. Territorial & monarchy-oriented developments – hardly human rights, 92

C.2. Capital/ material-oriented developments - human rights in prosperity, 94

      C.2.1. Agricultural economy, 94

      C.2.2. Industrial economy, 95

C.2.3. Service Economy, 97

C.2.4. Automated Economy, 98

C.2.5. Problems in capital models, 100

C.2.5.1. Demand, function of capital, 101
C.2.5.2. Capital must concentrate, 105
C.2.5.3. Capital must top profitability, 108
C.2.5.4. Capital must fluctuate, 111
C.2.5.5. The competition against itself, 113

C.3. Individual economy - global human rights, liberty and peace guarantee, 115

C.3.1. World-further prosperity in peace: AstronTimeOnomy and AstronSpaceOnouse Aspects, 117

C.3.2. Co-steering - swiveling freedom, 124

D. Index, 128

E. Short description, 130

F. The Trilogy, 133

G. Annex 1, 135

H. Space for notes, 137

A. Introduction

Space or room. Just search for "space, room" on the internet. Then look at the "pictures" for it. Mostly "chambers" are shown. Since the human brain thinks in pictures, the fact is: Most people think of an enclosed area at "space or room".

However, the room - or space - outside the above spatial vision is much larger: 50 billion light-years in diameter... And means: universe.

This is a perfect comparison to show how blind we go through our world. And how much potential there would be for everything if we only would have the "space" to look for. We might have it! We just need to leave our hamster wheel. Look outside the box. And think.

In the introduction-text of the book "AstronTimeOnomy" I wrote that the "own(!) time" can give the "power" to go ones´ own way. And I described how "time" can be used for this purpose. Each way, nevertheless, also needs "space". I bypassed this in the first book because it would have blown the frame there. I am catching up that now, in this book.

In order to make the earth sustainable for as long as possible, we need to implement new rules. As quickly as possible. Rules, that have fostered the 13.8 billion-year growth of universe. The most important is "energy" as such. But as well, the stabilizing, "time-outmaneuvering", aspects from the first book of this GlobalOnomy-trilogy (AstronTime-Onomy - with its focus on prosperity) shows possible optimization aspects. Additionally, there are the aspects on which we will focus in this book, AstronSpaceOnomy: freedom and peace. All possible correlations, will then be presented in the following book, Astron-EfficiencyOnomy (focus: welfare & sustainability). All this will help to optimize the world.

All books, train lateral thinking. The train to open eyes, to be curious, to get out of the hamster wheel. And train to see math, astronomy, economy, sociology, ecology and sustainability in a different way, than just focused on matter-aspects, as today. This helps to become more successful.

We will refine some additional dimensions and forces of "space" in this and the next book. Of course, parallel to other dimensions of other sectors..

"Space" seems to be one of the most important aspects of the universe. While the universe has "only" existed for 13.8 billion years in terms of "time-dimension", it has expanded to a diameter of 50 billion light-years in terms of "space-dimension". And it is still growing. And always growing faster.

But beware: the "variable" space in the universe - according to our new findings – is a variable "variable"… Space does not only have the 3 area dimensions (height, length, width). Space aspires to much more. More "value" than the pure 3-D aspects. The spatial aspects discussed in this current book, have the purpose of "going their own way" rather than "just" gaining 3-D-space.

The earthly, martial, materialistic and egoistic "area- expansion-striving" is, thus, rather "sub-optimal". At least, from an intellectual – and as well from a physical, astronomical optimization point of view. It also leads, time and again, to the collapse of powers. It is more worthwhile for mankind to optimize other(!) "space" aspects. Instead of investing money into weapons to conquer regions.

So, what is "space"? In this book we would like to give a rough cross-section of today's spatial considerations. We will also present our own inventions on "space". And what they mean for astronomy. Last, but not least, we will show how these astronomy aspects can be used as a guide to optimize our world as well.

B. SPACE: DIMENSIONS & VALUE IDEAS

B.1. General aspects of "space"

For most people, "space" or "room" is "only" correlated with a chamber. At least 90% of the pictures that the internet provides us for these words are: chambers. And since the brain thinks in pictures, the opening sentence applies.

Our "drawer thinking" (also a spatial dimension …) leads us to "store" something new (too) quickly into an existing drawer. Just, in order to quickly become "free" again for other (or for non-) thinking. So as not to have to be further involved about this new aspect. So as not to have to leave the comfortable path of the "known", the "status-quo". In order to remain in our hamster wheel. To continue with the same turns every day.

And with a big mass of drawers we build our own "room". We will increasingly block the windows and doors of this room, with all those drawers. So that at some point we will not see anything new anymore. No view of the surroundings from the previously existing openings. So that at some point we will not get out of our think-"houses" at all, any more, as even the doors are blocked with drawers. At a certain point we can no longer even "move" our own thoughts due to too much drawers barricading the space within our brains. We will lose our own "energy" generation ability. No new(!) thought may arise. We will surrender "blindly" to the existing drawer- system. Keep in the room, the prison, the hamster wheel. And we will fight against each new drawer (idea), as there is no place any more in our brain-chamber. Some of us by ignorance. Some of us in older days by amnesia. But as well, lamentably seldom, some lucky ones, not at all, until death.

The universe "thinks" different. At least it acts different: the strongest effort of the universe is to "expand" (at first glance). To achieve enough "space" for all "participants" and aspects. And all participants and aspects are "connected" by various forces (e.g.: matter, gravitation, centrifugal forces, energy, speed, space and time). But they are not stored in static drawers, forever and ever. Everything is relative (i.a. Albert Einstein's theories of relativity) – and thus open(!) to change.

And universe is not in a chamber (nor "nutshell"). Universe acts outside of our chamber-thinking. Continuously "expanding" and changing. However, we will relativize that "expansion" towards a special kind of "energy".

This openness, this energy (energy in astronomy means: "the power to do work"), this "commitment" towards "space"-"energy-" (and not matter- nor territory-)-achievement, seems to be one of the great differences between the more inefficient human activity-models and the enormous effectiveness of the universe "activities". If the universe were to operate primarily in our earthly "space" or size-extraction-dimensions, it might have collapsed long ago. Just as the "realms" of the Egyptians, Chinese, Greeks, Romans, Arabs, Spaniards, Portuguese, Danes, French, English, Germans, Russians, etc. collapsed.

I wanted to optimize sustainability, economy, sociology, ecology as well as freedom and peace in our world with the laws of astronomy. Thus, I searched in literature for the "formula for space". Negative report. There was(!) no formula for space as such. Despite the fact, that one of the greatest unknown forces seems to be hiding behind the "space": 73% of the unexplained forces concern the "dark energy": Why does the universe expand faster than it can be represented with today's formulas?!

"Space" also has many variants in our language usage: to achieve "free space(!)"; where there is a will, there is a "way(!)"; "drawer thinking". Freedom or peace also have a lot to do with (spiritual) "space".

But in the western - rather materialistic - orientation, our brain initially only sees "chambers". A stronger focus and change of consciousness on "free space" would also move mountains on our earth. Thinking outside the box, outside of the chamber, outside of the hamster wheel, helps. That is what will help towards new dimensions: new own(!) space – and as well: freedom and peace (enough "mental space", openness, in order to avoid "collisions", means wars).

Focusing on the (in our opinion) better: the "imaginary" power of (own) "space" (liberty, independency, own way) could reduce our "materialism" focus down to the level, that the "matter" has in the universe: 4.6% share of matter.

This is specially valid, as many of us 1) buy things, they don´t need, 2) with money, they don´t have, 3) to impress people they don´t like. This is no liberty. This is being prison of a vicious circle within a materialistic-orientated, box-thinker system.

"Liberty" (own space) will be generated by investing more time and more money in one's own knowledge, independence or in social commitment. And therefore, spending less time and less money for - often useless – products – and additionally the time to profile with them on the streets, to be seen ...

That would work very well for our "ambience", and as well, for ourselves.

B.2. General Earth aspects of space

The number of aspects related to space is immense. Investing in territorial expansion through wars, etc., not really makes sense. Humanity should consider, to invest in other aspects of space that promote prosperity, rather than just a territory-gain. Sure, with a territory, the size of (potential) "power" becomes visible at first glance. But only "size" - without internally enough "energy" (and all its sub-variants) and without a balanced "forces" ratio in the respective system - leads to the implosion of this territorial space, to a super-nova. In universe, the forces are balanced, if they e.g. correspond to the formulas of Albert Einstein. Human rights and an economy-rules usually ensure a balanced coexistence among people. However, if "togetherness" is too much claimed by only one side or dominated by only one aspect, the equation becomes unbalanced – and collapses in the medium term.

The following overview shows that space is many times more diverse than the 90% of the chambers, which we find on the internet:

1. Protection

Space provides shelter in caves, castles, houses, submarines, rockets, conservation vessels, ...

2. Orientation

Space aspects help to orientate within your perimeters: 1) devices (such as compass or

GPS), 2) maps, 3) nautical charts, 4) universe maps/images (such as those of Aristotle, the Church, Galileo, Newton, Einstein, Bright, etc.), ...

3. Storage

Space helps to store things in: warehouses, cellars, barrels, bottles, paper folders, purses and wallets, computer data storage, etc.

4. Speed

Space structuring brings efficiency: infrastructure (roads, rails, airports, power lines, internet lines or radio ranges, ...), ...

5. Architecture/Art

Space has infinite architectural manifestations (pyramids, churches, skyscrapers, mining mines, bridges, tunnels, ...) – not only chambers ...

6. Human aspects

Space plays a major role in human life-aspects: 1) without space, no life can arise or exist, 2) feel-comfortable at proximity or distance, 3) dream (spiritual space), 4) ideas (energetic "spark" – in the space of the brain), 5) own way (free space) ...

7. Economic aspects

Space also has economic dimensions: 1) customs duties at national borders, 2) parking fees, 3) rent / sale of 2-D m² surface or as 3-D: cm³ drinks in bottles ...

8. Technical aspects

Space has many technical aspects 1) Safety distance (warning systems – save lives); 2) workplace space-optimizations (increase productivity), 3) Air compression – in respiratory bottles to do research at difficult places, ...

9. Legal aspects

Space is extremely linked to legal aspects: 1) hunting grounds; 2) Country borders, 3) sea protection zones, 4) overflight rights, 5) "liberty" for interpretations, 6) (thoughts-) freedom, 7) free "space" to act, 8) peace – if everyone lets everyone think and go his way (mental space), ...

10. Environmental aspects

Without (free) space (existence "right") for nature, mankind also dies, …

11. Faith aspects

Faith-liberty or -repression has a lot to do with religions – or dictatorial constitutions, …

12. Mathematical dimension

Mathematics for the calculation of 2- or 3-dimensional spaces is one of the oldest disciplines (circle, sphere, triangle, pyramid, square, cube, etc. ...), …

13. Physical astronomical dimension

Space is an essential aspect and dimension for insights in astronomy. Especially in connection with its "counterpart", time, out of which speed results, …

14. Energetic dimension of space

Space has an energetic dimension, as will be shown later

15. Freedom dimension

However, the most important dimension for human aspects is the "free space", so that everyone can develop as he/she would like to do.

Our brain is a fascinating example of the space dimension. In the brain, much (also) is stored electronically. A huge storage (space) of knowledge. A "space" that exists physically and energetically. And not necessarily grows (physically), as knowledge (energetically) increases.

The more knowledge we incorporate, the better. Because knowledge is the basis for ideas – and the best basis for prosperity, stability, sustainability, transcendence, empathy, peace – and freedom.

15.1. Using the space formula as a basis for prosperity, freedom & peace on our earth.

In the universe, energy is the driving force. Energy is defined as "the power to do work". This, in physics, leaves it open, what kind of force is working and what kind of work is performed in each case. There are many types of constructive and destructive forces. In the universe, however, the "constructive" (* in our view - see below) forces seem to dominate. Because the universe uses most of its energy to "grow" (energetically, as we will show). And by doing so, it is achieving a lot of free "space" (in its energetic dimension) for its participants.

(* our view: In a democratic sense, "space", freedom, is viewed positively. And dictatorial centralism, is viewed as negative. Dictatorship acts like gravity, absorbs and destroys all in a black-hole, restricts space and liberty)

Our invented spatial formula tends towards the status of "energy" – and away from the status of "matter". Thus, with our inventions, Einstein's formula of the simple relativity theory ($E = m * c^2$) not only is a definition of a constant rule. A rule for the conversion of any matter into energy by means of a constant multiplier c^2. No, considered dynamically and extrapolated (according to our new formula complex - "hidden and

15

prohibited to think about ...") behind Einstein's formula there is also a dynamic process for the 5% matter(-energy) of space. We are gradually changing and supplementing Einstein's formula in this and the next book. And to this 5% energy-status-quo of the Einstein-know-how-era – we will be adding the missing 95% of – up to now - unexplored "dark energy" and "dark matter".

While Einstein & Co. discovered the heart-energy of universe – we are disclosing its brain-energy. While Einstein & Co. discovered the now, we will add the past and the future, dynamically, with our Dynamic-Relativity.

We will usher in a new era.

Denominating these enormous 95% of unknown forces as "dark" has nothing to do with "evil". It's just "non-visible", a little bit mysterious. Our brains also are in the dark. And we don't fear them. And here, as well, energy(-waves) is (are) the primarily "driving" factor(s). If we load energetically the material basis of our brain with knowledge and provide free "space" to explore new things, then a lot of prosperity will arise. Because the greatest asset of mankind is intelligence (energy) - and not the boring and dry figures of the GNP, the gross national product. With enough intelligence and wisdom, we will achieve the summit of the Maslow's Pyramid of Needs: transcendency, all of us. With intelligence, prosperity, transcendency, empathy, liberty, peace, welfare and sustainability will follow.

B.3. General universe aspects of space

The (free) space outside the enclosed area of the chambers in our brains is much larger than that of that room: it has a diameter of 50 billion light-years – and is called universe.

However, this diameter of 50 billion light-years is only the "visible" and "middle" area of the universe. Astronomy today divides the universe into three areas. Out of these, we only know the "middle area" a little bit better. The "central area" is that of the big bang. The actual status of research only reaches until a few seconds after the big bang. But the big bang itself – that area at the center of our model - has not yet been descrambled. And the "outer area" is the one we can't see with our telescopes. This, together with the ever-faster-moving-away stars, suggests that the "space" is infinite – in the outside of the 3rd area.

None of these three universe areas is encased in stable "walls". Nevertheless, there are other forms of "being" in the three areas. At its core (and in the middle), it's about strings, quanta, electrons, etc. The middle range is our current one. We understand it in terms of some forces (as energy, velocity) and matter (as stars and planets). And for the external sphere, there are many assumptions, but no evidence.

The middle range seems to grow dynamically, seemingly limitless. And it is growing at a rate that, according to today's astronomy formulas, cannot really be. The forces behind it are called "dark energy" within the astronomy discipline. "Dark" because you cannot define these energetic forces – at least not with existing astronomy formulas. However, since this is about 72% of the energy "composition"[*2] of the universe, we were very interested in this dimension…. And we discovered quite some correlations.

The second very large sector, to which no answers have(had) yet been found, is the spatial movement of suns and planets around their respective galaxy/star center. Actually, this should be faster, but something in space seems to slow this down. This braking force affects 23% of space. And because it is unknown, it is called "dark matter". Because gravity (matter) is similarly braking.

Lee Smolin*[1] wrote about "space": "Nothing is more commonplace than space, but if we examine it more closely, there is nothing more mysterious." Such sentences are both, a challenge and an incentive for lateral thinkers like us... 😊

When it comes up to "fast" or "slow", time aspects always play a role.

Stephen Hawking's*[3] quotation about "time": "... **time (whatever that** may be) ..." sounds no less mysterious. However, Albert Bright*[4] has already solved this mystery in the book "AstronTimeOnomy".

Considering the statements - concerning both of the above-mentioned "dark" forces - we can state, that they have only limitedly to do with time. For the solution of 95% of the astronomical composition, therefore, certain correlations need to be considered more deeply.

It is interesting, however, to state here, that Einstein's & Co. inventions "only" are concerning roundabout 5% of the universe. With the perspective of 95% unknown aspects, of course, it brings all the more opportunities and enthusiasm to embark on a new research path.

First of all, however, it is a pity that astronomy does not have a formula for such a central size as "space". We actually wanted to get a "mathematically based" space-formula, for why the universe grows better than many aspects on our earth. And then we wanted to apply this formula to various earthly aspects and challenges. These are such as economic growth, market share gains − or like: why aggressive states, after they have reached a certain territorial size through invasions, they repeatedly collapsed.

With a similar mental wit background, we searched for a time formula in 2014. The astronomical dimension "time" seemed to be the most useful to look after, for a better money system − based on astronomy laws.

"Matter" as currency basis, has already failed on Earth (at least) once, with i.a. the gold standard.

Gravity and centrifugal force did not seem to be appropriate enough to us, because they were only secondary aspects, in correlation with matter.

Time, that would have been ideal ... . In 2016 we published the book "AstronZeitOnomie" (AstronTimeOnomy in 2021). With the time formula in mind (shown among others in "AstronZeitOnomie"), we came up with ideas for a new currency and economic system.

Since then, we have been hoping to find something that could optimize this invented economy and money model, which we "constructed" with the "time" dimension.

Something that could enrich this system with even more "life-power". Even more, as, since the strongest endeavor of universe seems to be to create "space" for all involved aspects.

And, all the more, because in this aspect, "finding space for all", on earth, it is not really progressing. Concentration is processing on a materialistic 3-D-basis. And not, as in the universe, "energetic" freedom, "expansion" .

Capital-centralized-power is at a level, rarely seen before.

The risk that these system concentrations, lead to a bursting of the bubble (a super nova with a black hole) – and then plunge the entire system into a crisis – this danger is very great at the moment, because of:

a) the results or rotation (i.a. profit/year or speculative-profit/second) needs to get faster and faster. No longer 3-year targets for sales, but nano-seconds for speculation, are needed.
This leads to the (at the moment, still stabilizing) environment of employees, being "thrown off course" (industry 4.0). This is due to the centrifugal force (i.a. via faster machines) of the central system (invested capital). Employees are thrown out of (their) orbits, as machines work faster.

b) the size of the bubble (and the often accompanying, over-bureaucratization) makes everything slack. As well, it is no longer possible to "reverse the route" nor "to brake in time" (see as well all the bailouts for states, banks, insurance companies, ...) or/and

c) systems are getting bigger and bigger and absorbing the entire periphery like a black-hole (all means and energies available are absorbed – under the political motto "too big to fail"). Thus, the "breathable air" is being taken away from the periphery ...

In the book AstronTimeOnomy, we have found a way for the periphery to fly past the shabby system mentioned above. Through enough self-energy. Just as you may fly past a "black hole" in universe without getting devoured, by accelerating to the speed of light.

However, that what could complete this picture, was still missing: a formula for the "space". A formula that would "expand" things on earth like universe is "expanding": energetically. And defying all super-nova and black holes.

In the book AstronTimeOnomy, however, it is also clear that we humans (especially in industrial worlds) are very materially- and time-driven. Interestingly, according to our calculations, matter concentration is always associated with time concentration, as well in universe .... Interestingly, there are a lot of evidences in the universe. Shortly (380,000 years) after the big bang[2] – the proportion of "dark matter" was very large: 63% - and thus at that time also the proportion of the destructive/ hostile "time dimension". Our world today - with its primary matter/ time orientation - seems to be at the level of the beginnings of the universe ...! But that was 13,799,620,000 years ago (13.8 billion minus 380,000). May be, it is time for a mental change?!

Today, 13.8 billion years after the big bang, the proportion of "dark matter" has fallen to 23%[2] and the share of "dark energy" increased from zero to 72%[2] . One of the key differences from the origin is the "available" space of today. That is why we suspected within that mysterious dimension of space a force, a formula. The rest was hard work, lateral thinking, all the own setbacks and defending against foreign attacks of dissidents, in order to survive – and save the ideas ☺ .

B.4. General relativity aspects of space

"Space" is relative. And the relativity of the universe ends (according to today's tendency - at least at one of the "ends" or "borders") in "space", as we will show. In extrapolated space. In a space, ahead of its 3-D-dimension, in which we are used to "see" the space.

While we today still land on the Mars with Newton's formulas, a navigation system on Earth would not work exactly enough without Einstein's relativity. But these calculations are mainly based on the actual situation of solar systems or galaxies. They do not consider, that the forces of time and space change within time. One initial sign of this is shown to us, when comparing time at 2 identical clocks, one at the top of a big mountain - and one at the bottom. Time runs faster at the top. This means, that time is relative. And if time is relative, space as well must be relative, as it has a close correlation with time. Both components, time and space, are currently mainly used as "measures", as no formula has (had …) been developed for them so far.

B.4.1. Relativity examples of time:

Time (measured by 2 identical clocks) runs slower at sea level than on a mountain of the same planet. The stronger the gravity, the stronger the effect. This effect is called "the twins paradox"[*5]. This paradox is no paradox anymore, if gravity- and speed- aspects are considered at the corresponding places. But this is only valid for the actual situation and time constellations. But does not consider, that time goes on – and space grows stronger.

Yes, this also makes sense when looking with the eyes of our invented formula for time. The destructive effect of time is stronger at the shore than on the mountain. Time, as a force, is more intensely at the shore. And since the times "material portion" (and thus the laming gravity) are more intense here, time here seems to be (technically measurable) slower. And can destroy more with its special constellation.

But the "twin paradox" is only valid at todays constellation. In future the effect of the "twin paradox" will be stronger. These are things, we added to the actual know-how, by inventing the formulas of time and space. Time and space as such, and not only as scales, measure-units, to calculate with.

Both, gravitational and time-effect increases, are destructive. Gravity because its extremum, black hole, destroys everything. The time because its extrapolation to the maximum-extreme leads to a division by zero – which is "nothing", is less than death. When "the clocks stand still" when a star no longer rotates, when the centrifugal force extinguishes or becomes too low, the gravitational and time waves gain in size and strength and destroy everything.

B.4.1.1. Conclusions of the twin paradox*5

We can't confirm the conclusion in literature*6. Considering our formula of time, we can't confirm that the slowly running clocks at the shore lead to longer lives. Neither mathematically*4 nor in real life: Most people who get very old without modern life-support medicine do not live at the sea level, but in elevated areas.

The gravitational and time waves can be imagined by dropping a stone into calm water. Right next to the incursion point, large waves form, which (if it were a large comet in the sea) would destroy everything in the immediate vicinity. The further away these waves move, the smaller they become and the more their destructive power diminishes.

The clocks run slower at the see-level. This is because of the gravitational pull at sea level (which, again, led to the classification of time as being relative). However, all this is done only as a correlation to gravitation and not with a time- (nor space-) formula(s). Although the clock runs slower at the sea side, people live shorter(!), the stronger the gravity is – and not(!), as quoted, living longer at the seaside. However, this result from reality and from our formulas is only indirectly corelated to gravity. Much more, it is a result of the respective time "carrying" matter and the energy present there – in combination with the forces of the environment (for more information, see B.4.2.).

B.4.2. Relativity examples of space:

Alternatively, if the mountain twin lives in a spaceship that moves through space at almost the speed of light, the spaceship twin returns much younger than the twin brother left at the shore-side of the origin planet. This is also correct according to our research, because then the negative effect of time (and gravity) is decimated. And / or the positive effect of space (and energy) is potentiated. At (almost) the speed of light, life can become (almost) infinite.

Also from this space/speed view, the twin brother would live longer on the mountain - even if the time of the "technical" clock runs faster there (the individual destructive "waves" of time are weaker (the time – and also the clock - runs faster, but time has less effect, because the amount of energy (speed) and "space"-forces have increased – and that of matter (gravity) has decreased. At the summit of the mountain, the centrifugal force (and thus also the speed and the energy out of speed and space) are greater than at sea level – and the gravitational and time force are smaller.

All this shows that space (as well as our formula of time) must also be relative. While Albert Einstein made enormous insights with the relative space/time, this was "only" (sorry) "general correlations", measures or gradients, general findings based on location comparisons, which were defined and explained by his general relativity. It was already discovered that time and space must be relative! But we were interested more in depth: we wanted the concrete "formulas" of space and time as such...

So: There is a contradiction even within that quoted paragraph*6. The example: After a long trip (far away from gravity) at light-speed of the 1st twin, he comes back and is younger than the 2nd twin, that had stayed on earth. So, although time runs faster at the top of the hill (far away from gravity), now, at the second example, he comes back younger?! That makes no sense.

And: Einstein´s aspect of general relativity, that there is a dependance as well, on how someone is moving, works for this example.

But: It "only" (sorry) considers the actual status of galaxies. Thus, it "maximally" can explain the 5% of matter correlated aspects, of universe. "Maximal", because general relativity can´t explain "dark matter" (23% of all energetic forces in universe: Why do planets not orbit faster around their stars?). And this aspect concerns the "now", the actual status of galaxies.

And/but: General relativity, as well, does not explain "dark energy" (72% of all energetic forces in universe: Why does universe grow faster, than we can calculate?)

The solution?: All examples (mountain/coast, light-speed-voyage and the remaining 95% of universe forces) cope with each other, when considering our formulas for time, space and dynamic-relativity.

So, Isaac Newton relativized the absolute position in space[*5] (but had no space formula). Albert Einstein relativized absolute time (but had no formula for time). And we, with our a) formula of "time" (volume 1), b) formula of "space" (volume 2, this book) and c) formula of "dynamic-relativity" (volume 3) can relativize all. As well the up to now remaining un-known forces of "dark matter" and "dark energy". That´s a new model of universe ... ☺

B.5. Other astronomical aspects of space

B.5.1. The astronomical "image" of space

In astronomy, space plays a major role. By observing the movements of the stars and planets within space it is possible to measure many aspects and discover correlations. Space is primarily used for measurement, as a yardstick. And although the "meter" is of course also present here, measuring in light years is more common, because of the enormous size of the universe. The universe has a diameter of 50 billion light-years.

However, we want to "penetrate" into the depths of space (not 3-D-, not space-time- nor space-curvature-like, but as a pure formula). To do so, we first try to "make a picture" (or several images) of what is happening there, outside, in the universe, with space. We then want to develop a formula from this.

Space is the best dimension to represent the diversity of relativity. Before the big bang, there seemed to be nothing. Therefore, apparently, neither room. The big bang is a singular event that has not been reconstructed to this day. One thing is certain: without space, this explosion could not have taken place. Because an explosion needs space. With the explosion, the energy used the space to spread. At first, only the energy of the big bang was created. Only the left side of Albert Einstein's equation of simple relativity: the energy, E. But space must have been "included" in this E. Astronomers define E, energy, as "the power to do work".

We should add here: "The power **and the space** to do work", "The force **and the space** to do work".

Then time, speed, matter, gravity, centrifugal force ... developed. And with, among other things, matter, the optical 3-D-dimensions of space (length, width, height) developed. Since energy and matter are the primary visible aspects, astronomy was primarily oriented towards them. Although matter in universe only has a 4.6% of "importance" (energy power share). This also limits the amount of forces (energy), that can be determined so far by formulas. Limited to mainly: matter. This applies to both: to the Simple Relativity Theory and to the General Relativity Theory by Albert Einstein. Both formulas affect 4.6% of the total forces of the universe. An unknown force, 23%, is about why the planets do not orbit their star faster than they should be able to do according to current calculations. And the greatest unknown force are the 72% that cause the universe to grow more quickly than it "should" be able to do.

In order to approach the subject – and also knowing that the brain thinks (or wants to think) in pictures, we have started to draw. This helped us to approach the mathematical physical thoughts of our idols. And also helped us to design new (space) "pictures" and "constructions". Then we tried to reproduce and prove them with mathematical physical astronomical formulas.

An explosion cannot take place without space. At a bomb-explosion, most people only see the bomb (matter) that explodes. Then the light that arises from the explosion (energy). And then the damage (matter) resulting from the explosion. The space used for this is ignored because it is a minor point, an implicitness, something, that is there and that we do not have to care about. The universe, however, fights tirelessly for a central "need": space. And space is the dimension in which universe "invests" most of its energy (72%). And which, up to now could not be unmasked ...

The big-bang. No bang without space ...

The black hole – no light with no space …

Even if the photons of light as such have no material dimension, the light can only act as light, when it hisses through space. No light without space.

Where extreme concentrations of gravity and time predominate, space is displaced. Due to the lack of space, light has no possibility for expansion. We do not see light in extreme black holes. Gravity should not be able to "swallows" the light, because photons have no "material dimension". The lack of space – due to the power of time, and not the gravity, prevents the expansion of light at black holes.

Energy to matter. No space, no matter …

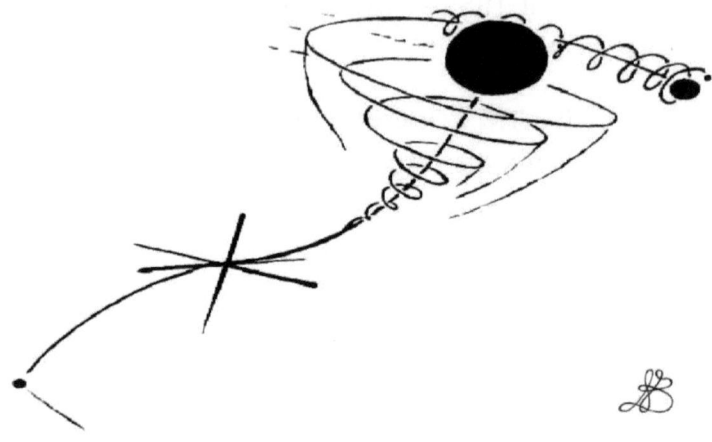

Space is also required for the transformation of energy into matter – and its expansion.

And with the glowing matter and the resulting light - as the only "visible" - came the material orientation, the matter-focus of mankind, although matter in the universe has only an importance of 4.6%. Space was transparent. Thus, nobody really cared about it.

Space has mainly been used as a scale. But its meaning or / and power was never recognized. It is just, as Lee Smolin writes: "Nothing is more commonplace than space, but if we examine it more closely, there is nothing more mysterious." *1

The Universe – no space, no expansion …

The universe. 50 billion lightyears in diameter – and we know only 4.6%.

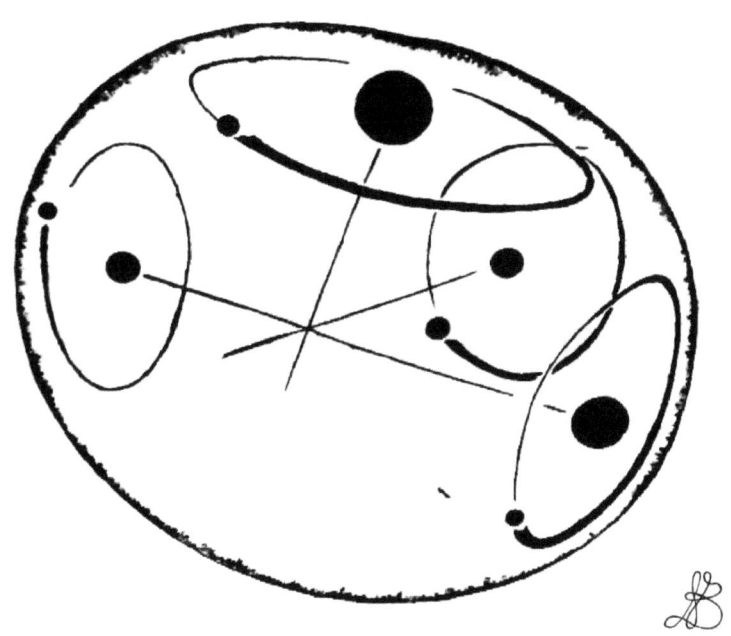

Human beings primarily think in pictures and believe their eyes more than their ears. And unfortunately, often, as well more than their knowledge. And since materialistic aspects could not explain many things, much was assigned to the divine. In order to store this again "materially" in a drawer of the brain, huge magnificent churches and colorful paintings (the latter initially primarily for church purposes) were created.

The free "space" for not only ecclesiastical images and thoughts, is very young.

Galileo Galilei was excommunicated because of his space thoughts around 1500 AD – and only rehabilitated by the Catholic Church in 1992(!).

The "established status-quo" in the time of Albert Einstein led to the founding of the "Association of astronomers against the theories of Albert Einstein". Fortunately, it was not the association, but Einstein, who received the Nobel Prize.

The free space for one's own thinking and actions, however, is far from being reached –

and unfortunately only granted to those who have enough energy (capital or/and own "power") to assert themselves against all the inertness and adversities of drawer-thinkers within the "established status quo".

In the course of history, a wide variety of "images" of the universe, its stars, planets and spatial aspects emerged:

THE EARTH AS A DISC

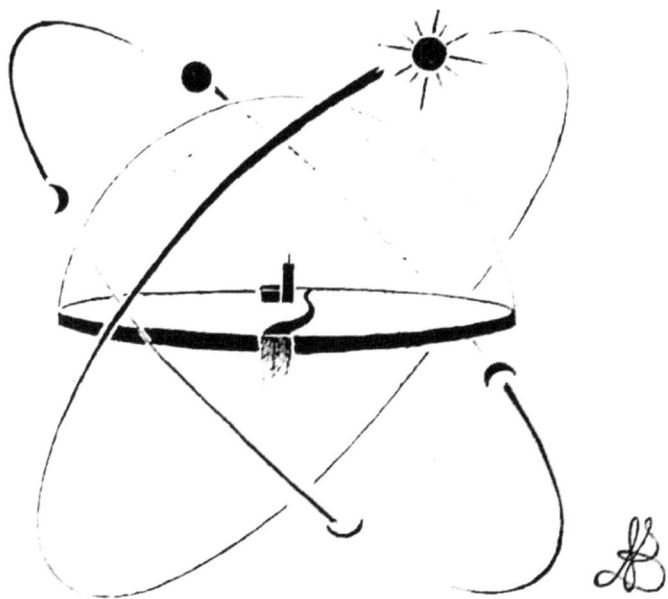

For the Christian Church, the earth was the center of the universe and everything revolves around it, with the earth being only a disc. And you might fall to hell at its border.

GALILEO AND NEWTON GRAPHIC

Galileo Galilei discovered that it is not the earth but the sun that is the center of our star system. And that many planets, including the earth, were orbiting this sun. Isaac Newton discovered gravity and centrifugal force. And also defined them as the central forces for the coexistence of planets and stars:

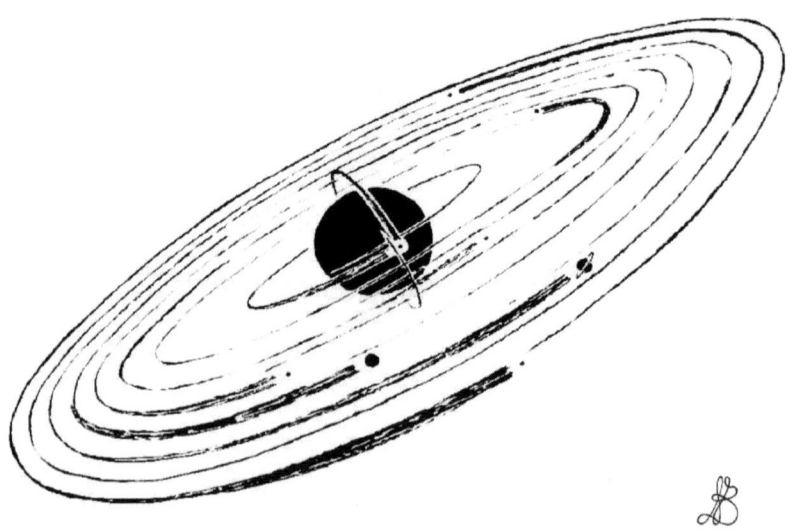

EINSTEIN WAVES GRAPHIC

Albert Einstein not only relativized many forces and matter in the universe with his "simple" relativity theory. With his "general" theory of relativity, he also rejected Newton's idea of correlation for the coexistence of stars and planets. From now on, each planet has its own path (orbit), which results, among other things, from its space-absorbing force. And it positions its own orbit where the space-absorbing force of its star (weakening with increasing distance) corresponds to the planet's own space-absorbing force. Therefore, the planets "float" around their star at different wave-strengths/ waves:

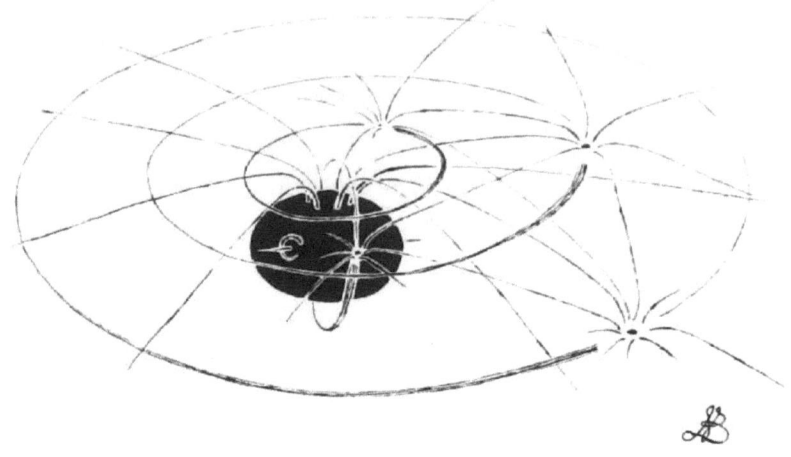

After discovering the formulas of time and space, however, we no longer believe in Albert Einstein's "space-absorption" nor in "curved space". In the following we want to "draw" a new picture of the universe.

THE NEW ALTERNATIVE PICTURES OF UNIVERSE...

1) TIME-forces as 1st part of an explanation of our alternative space-model.

Based on our discovered time-formula*4 we can define as a context that the orbits of planets (around their star) or stars (around their galaxy center) expand in the course of development (time). This is valid as long as the central star grows – so its time "shield" grows like inflating a ball - and displaces space:

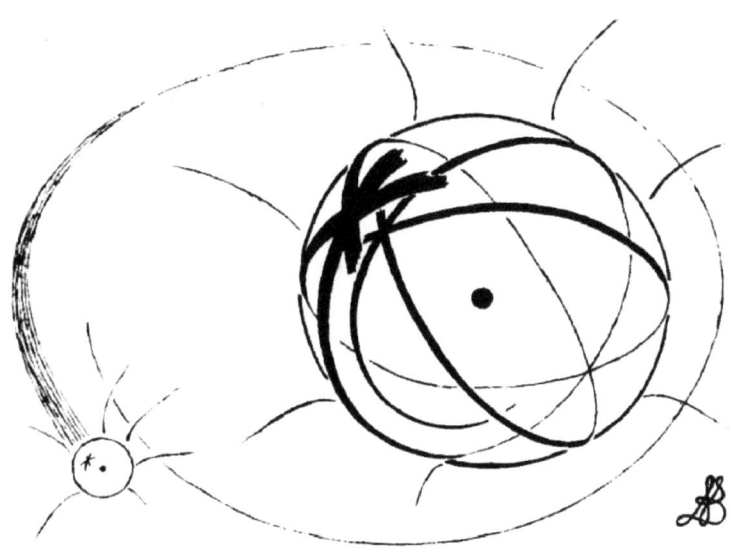

All stars first grow by conversion of gas into matter – and later, when they are too big or the remaining energy is too low, they shrink by an implosion, a super nova. This will also happen to our sun – in about 5 billion years. Then it will have reached 4 times its current size.

During growth, the material portion (i.a. initially helium formation) increases – and the energy component decreases (a lot of energy is released by hydrogen nuclear fusion). The destructive time "shell" gradually increases its power. It gradually displaces the liberal forces of space. It grows like the casing of a snail. And material portion, with less energy grows. Even worse, energy losses – automatically lead to inertia, as well by increasing gravity. Increasing gravity also suppresses more and more its "counter-pole", the centrifugal force*[14]. And, at some point, the star implodes into a super nova.

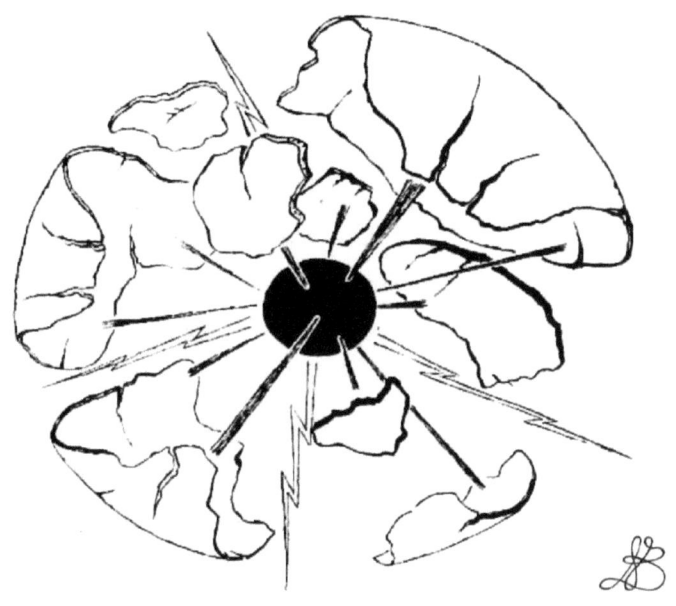

What happens after a super-nova is not clear. It essentially depends on the size of the original star. The larger, the more likely a "black hole" will emerge. If the sun "only" disintegrates, then the entire matter transforms into energy. The time "shell" also breaks. It breaks along with its time-"carrying" matter. Along with the ex-star. Imploding from the outside to the inside. The "time has come": the sun dies.

Gravity and time disappear if everything disintegrates and no black hole is created. Energy and space then gain strength again, because no disturbing time shield of the star is "in the way" anymore.

Quasar

However, sometimes a remnant of the star remains as matter. This is highly concentrated. The strength of the gravitational and time waves increases proportionally (comparing the new size of the quasar to the old size of the star). But they are smaller overall, since a part of the matter has turned into energy during implosion. Further energy is thrown into the universe as rays. At some point, however, this quasar also breaks due to the strength of its own gravity and time power – probably also because more and more energy is thrown into the universe from the existing residual matter via two rays. Gravitation seems to be so strong, that the energy is squeezed out of the remaining matter. "The time has come" for this quasar to die as well.

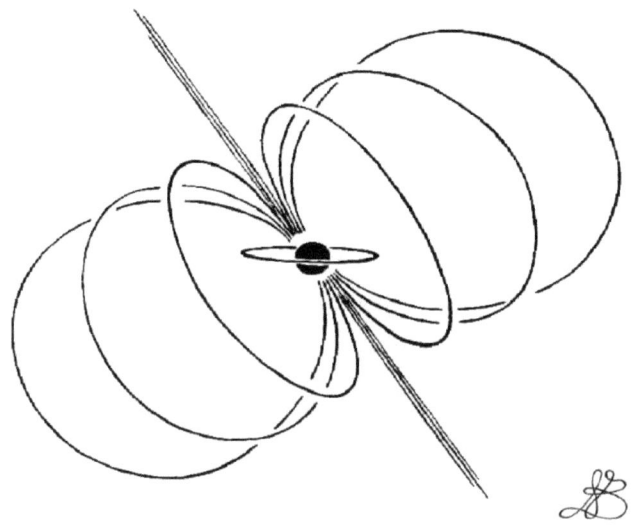

BLACK HOLE

However, if the star turns into a black hole after its super-nova implosion, not only the gravity of the original star is preserved. This black hole also increases its size by "absorbing" many other comets and planets around the former star. And all energies of all implosions are also absorbed. Even light can be "absorbed" at an extreme black-hole-constellation. With no remaining matter, no time will exist anymore, neither. Therefore, the forces of space will disappear as well, as both are correlate with each other by multiplication (as we will show later). Without space-energy as a stabilizing power not only light has no place to go anywhere any more. But as well many of the old planets of the surroundings will die. Formally they were orbiting (as well) on their space-energy balance. The balance with the space-energy of their star at their orbit-site. But now they "slip" into the gravitational "crater" of the black hole and are decomposed there into "nothingness". Neither matter nor energy nor time nor space – at least not in their "origin" status – will exist there anymore.

2) SPACE forces as the 2nd part of an alternative model of universe.

The space of a chamber is limited. But it allows us to survive in winter. And we enjoy the space in nature in the summer. But the limitation by the protective shield of our atmosphere is so far away that we unfortunately hardly pay attention to it. At least, we, in no way, preserve it in a similar way, as we do for our visible chamber walls. If this continues, "the ceiling (the sky) will fall on our heads". We will expose ourselves to the destructive forces within universe.

Space has a value. Life-preserving space is worth investing. Houses and atmosphere-shell. Both need continuous value-keeping and renovation "energy". The Universe itself, invests most of its energy into the "space"-dimension, in order to "grow" and "survive". With enough "space" for each planet and star, major crises are much less common, than they occur again and again on Earth.

Space in the universe, however, is not primarily three-dimensional space, even if its "obvious" "greatness" may give this impression. Space, according to our findings, seems to be primarily a force, something like energy. The fact, that the space of the universe is expanding so rapidly cannot be understood with current mathematics. Therefore, this expansion force was also called "dark energy". This dark energy accounts for 72% of all the forces of the universe.

But if the space-force accounts for 72% of the forces of the universe, then it cannot be, that planets or stars might be able to bend space. Especially not, since the matter of the universe accounts for only 4.6% of all the energy. We therefore assume that Albert Einstein's theories regarding space curvature are not correct.

Space has - and is - a force, has a function and a value. We will specify these dimensions with the formula in the next chapter.

B.6. The space formula

We invented the formula of time (see book: AstronTimeOnomy*⁴) because we were searching for an equivalent dimension for "money" (of our earthly economic systems*¹²) within astronomy. We were looking for something with a similar function in universe. This might be working better than money on earth. And might be transferable to earth constellations. We were sure that time is the best size to be analyzed. However, since there was no formula for the "time" as such (Stephen Hawking: "Time, WHATEVER THAT may be ...*³), we invented a formula. We have also been able to transfer its central effects towards the world's economy and prosperity.

The economic model we designed in the book AstronTimeOnomy is based on a big financial opportunity. This enables every person to pursue the profession which is most important to him. We have succeeded in the financial model for this. But in order to be able to really implement this – and to be able to generate growth, we lacked something. Again, we searched for central variables in the universe. That the universe has been growing for 13.8 billion years - and still is growing, even faster - is an indication that it is doing slightly better than humanity. The forces of these unknown forces add up to 72% of all energy in the universe. That's the kind of challenge we were looking at. We needed a potential spatial formula that might be transferred to humanity and earth aspects. But the status-quo formulas with their variables finally were no choice, as non was able to define, why the universe grows so fast. What a surprise. The same as when searching for the time formula. We had to realize that there was no formula for the space as such, neither.

We were definitely sure, that "space" as such might be a solution. There is more 3-D-room for expansion in space than there is on Earth. Thus, we needed something ahead of the 3-D-dimension, something energetic .... Something, where accumulation does not automatically lead to additional 3-D-space. We needed something, that generates energy without additional space. Something like the free space in our brains. Something, that might be charged with know-how (to improve wealth via knowledge and wisdom) without expanding our head-sizes. And without improving own wealth via conquering others territories. We needed space as energy. Again, we landed at Albert Einstein as a basis, to start going ahead.

We developed the space formula on the same basis on which we had already developed the time formula. We defined the c of Einstein's simple relativity formula ($E = m*c^2$) as speed (and did not just consider it as a constant). Speed (also) results from the longitude (space) travelled within a certain time (like: km/s). We solved Einstein's formula towards the spatial aspect of velocity (space). And we supplemented (new definitions) or shortened (excluding variables by defining them as constants) some aspects, in order to achieve the necessary focus on "space":

$E = M * c^2$ M (matter in capital) to be able

to distinguish from m (meter)

To view space in a differentiated way …
- I expand the formula to add the components "behind" the light-speed (the c^2): space and time:

$E = M * (300{,}000 \text{ km/s})^2$

$E = M * \dfrac{(300.000*1000 * m)}{s}^2$

To view space in an exposed way
- I use a constant for the time:

$z = \dfrac{300.000.000}{s}$

$E = M * (z * m)^2$,   taking the root …

$\sqrt{E} = \sqrt{M} * (z * m)$,   dividing by $\sqrt{M}$ …

$\dfrac{\sqrt{E}}{\sqrt{M}} = z * m$,   divided by z …

$$m = \frac{(\sqrt{E}\ )}{(\sqrt{M}\ )}\ /\ z$$

as z and √ are always constant aspects, for simplicity, it can also be said:

SPACE = ENERGY / MATTER

Space has an energetic and a material part.

There is also space in every matter.

Space seems to be (also) an energetic force. It also must have something like "energy waves" as a form of appearance.

Since matter - according to Einstein - can also be energy, the above correlation is also conceivable. That the result of this will then be "space" is surprising. It takes a while to get used. But we will prove by several aspects.

The room:

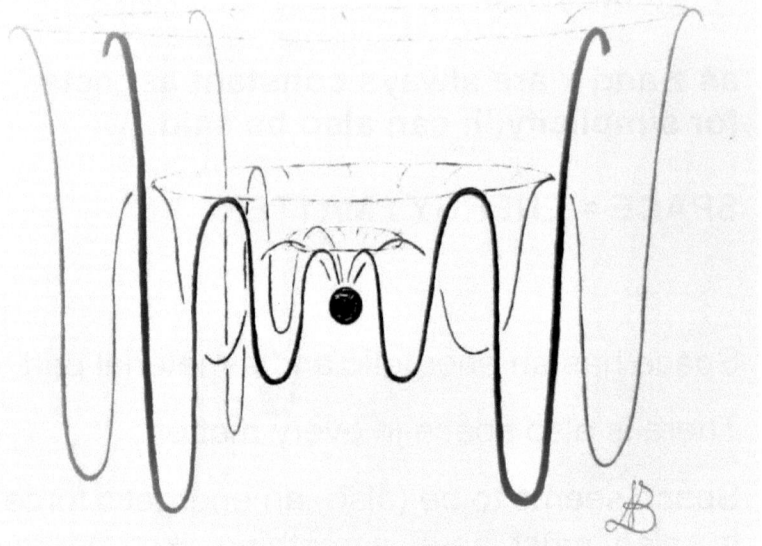

B.7. Justification for the speed approach with the "constant": "c² "

The most severe negative criticism we received from the invention of the time formula is that the "c²" of Einstein's Simple Theory of Relativity ($E = m * c^2$) is a "constant". It was determined by many experiments. It has nothing to do with speed. Although the "c" usually stands for the speed of light, the constant "c" is squared. It is just purely randomly the square of that number(!), that casually correspond to the "speed of light". By multiplication with c^2 one can calculate the energy content from each matter. Nothing more nor less. And: as light-speed already is the quickest speed possible, a squared light speed makes no sense at all.

B.7.1. Derivation justification for the space and time formulas – taken differently

When we developed our formulas, we used as much as possible existing(!) and verified(!) formulas. We then combined them with our lateral thinking, to come up with new thoughts. Verified knowledge is the best basis for new ideas and wisdom. This helps to have as few as possible policy discussions. But also, for not having to break too much thinking-barriers due to the drawer thinking. This as well is present at established scientists and institutions. Arguing with established formulas helps to at least be able to achieve some first discussion steps ...

I always do research on my own, for myself, so as not to be blocked at the first approaches towards new ideas. And I have already thought of other things with and about the time and space formulas. Things, that are much further than they are depicted in these first two books. I know that my approaches can solve many unanswered questions. And I have discovered, overcome and corrected many dead ends, mistakes and even only apparent errors during the formula developments. I learned that even factual mathematics can also be viewed differently. And interpretations may be endless …

But I couldn't let it happen, that my approaches were to be suffocated at the beginning. Although I solved unresolved issues, scientists told me that this was just coincidence, but was not scientifically relevant in any way, since the base was already not "allowed". My barriers are not (yet … because probably still too unknown ...) a) the church (although so far time and space are marketed as something divine), nor b) the nobility nor c) the anti-Einstein association. My barriers are the established scientists, with their institutionalized, formalistic approach to knowledge, being "allowed" only at professor titles. And as well their thinking-barriers. And also, their quantity. The last can in no way do justice to the growing knowledge. Knowledge doubles every 2 to 3 years. The number of professors does not. Purely for reasons of time, they have to fend off anything that does not come from their circles. And due to lack of time, many things, even in those holy circles, do not fulfil requirements. So much things go wrong, that a new "Einstein-Organization" was founded in the USA, to define new rules for scientific work … . But: Formalism is a big enemy of innovation.

Thus, I am all the more grateful that there are such institutions as the Patent Office and its sub-institutions, like VG-Wort. And worldwide cooperating libraries and knowledge preserving commitments. Here my approaches have been adopted as original and unique. And VG-Word pursues and calculates fees for each citation of my approaches. The same is valid for systems of top-publishers, like BoD, Books on Demand. With Albert Einstein´s experience with the "Association against the ideas of Albert Einstein", we see how important these neutral institutions are. Because the "rest of the world" often encloses itself in its "thinking drawers". To avoid everything new.

Nevertheless, as my extensions to the Einstein formula seem to be "not permissible" for the "established institutions" (at least not those, where I had the chance to speak with), I must use other formulas that have already been officially recognized by "them". To win against them with their own weapons. To justify my ideas and actions. Purely for the sake of form. Formalisms, that rob my time. But: since I am a lateral thinker, I was sure that at some point I would find a basis that would "legalize" my thoughts afterwards. Or I might develop something "scientifically and formalistically correct" by myself. That would consume much time. But for me, the results of my researches were so clear that I knew I was on the right track. I was sure that at some point I would be able to find a proof with "official formulas".

I've found what I've been looking for. Thanks to a book about physics and astronomy, which my two sons gifted to me. And yet I had to think a little "cross" and "tinker" a bit, to get things the right way.

The solution is called "deformation work" and is a subcategory of "inelastic kick" taking into account that "speeds in opposite direction are negative" *⁹. Got it?! 🙂 . I never thought, that proves for my cross-thinking might be so hidden.

Sounds crazy, but: I wanted to use the photons (quantum particles) of the light and let them bounce against each other - at the speed of light. I was looking for a formula, which tells me something about the velocity of two objects bouncing together. Do the 2 velocities just add or are they theoretically squared, when colliding? If velocity squares, then Einstein´s c^2 may be used as velocity of energy when light bounces against light from opposite sides. That was an idea within a dream at night. I took note and researched the next morning… . Cross-thinking always leads you on new paths …

However, photons have no mass, so the "m's" of the equation could not be "stocked".

And the found formula was not adding velocities, for what I was looking for. The result of that formula was energy resulting from the collision. Energy??? Energy!!!

Why not let planets or rockets collide at the speed of light? This becomes difficult, because it is hardly possible to use so much energy for speed. At least not with the formulas that exist today, in order to get matter achieving the speed of light. (With my thoughts on "dark energy" it is very possible to achieve this – see next book, volume 3). Nevertheless: on the one hand, approximation values are enough for me. And on the other hand, that found formula is abstract enough to be able to represent this too.

However, it is a new, mathematically "factual", "interpretation" … of Einstein's Simple Relativity Theory. Because it is not about the energy-"gain" from one(!) particular matter. But it is about the energy-"loss" in a collision of two(!) matter masses. However, it comes down to the same, it´s about "E" … :

The "inelastic shock":

Really Fascinating … 😊 …

m1   Mass of the body 1

m2   Mass of the body 2

v1   Speed of the body 1

v2   Speed of the body 2

V   common speed of both bodies after impact

E1   Sum of the energy, energies of both bodies before impact

E2   Sum of the energy, energies of both bodies after impact

ΔE   Energy loss = deformation work: W

$$W = E1 - E2 = \frac{m1 * m2}{2(m1 + m2)} \times (v1 - v2)^2$$

However, since it is one of the masses with opposite direction, minus becomes plus:

$$W = E1 + E2 = \frac{m1 * m2}{2(m1 + m2)} \times (v1 + v2)^2$$

Since both masses fly at the speed of light …:

$$W = E1 + E2 = \frac{m1 * m2}{2(m1 + m2)} \times (c+c)^2$$

Or:

$$W = E1 + E2 = \frac{m1 * m2}{2(m1 + m2)} \times 2\,c^2$$

2 can therefore be striked out - i.e.:

$$W = E_1 + E_2 = \frac{m_1 * m_2}{(m_1 + m_2)} \times c^2$$

When inserting the values for the matter, one comes to a value of the total matter "M"

And when the two E's are added, a total E is obtained:

$$W = E = M * c^2$$

This corresponds to Einstein's Simple Relativity Theory... ☺

If the physicists who calculated the energy on impact had had the idea and the courage to think in light-speed dimensions, they could have developed Einstein's formula before Einstein.

If Einstein would have had in mind this formula and our cross-thinking mix, he would not have had to do so much experimentation to get the c^2 for his "Simple Relativity Theory".

c^2 has also something to do with SPEED, SPACE and TIME. Therefore, all my thoughts are on a realistic basis!!! And should no longer be forbidden!!! ☺.

B.8. (Cross) correlations – as SPACE formula justification

Correlations help to understand things. The consideration of aspects from different plate edges brings alternative solutions or/and confirmation of assumptions or findings.

The above formula suggests to us that c^2 - based on the equation for the inelastic shock - could well be interpreted as speed. But: there is nothing faster than the speed of light at the moment. Thus, the c^2 should not really be interpreted "only" as "speed". Speed initially only was a tool for us. But behind our combination of space and time formulas there are hidden also other forces, not just speed. Therefore, we will look for further aspects and evidences that make our new space formula - as such - plausible. Here it helps to look at parallel, correlation aspects. This allows to see things more neutrally.

B.8.1. Correlation between energy, matter and gravity

If you ask what someone knows about Albert Einstein, immediately there comes a formula:

$E = m * c^2$, the "Simple Relativity Theory".

But the resulting energy represents only 5% of the total energy within the universe. Einstein was clear about that. Perhaps that is why he tried to find a part of the missing energy (about 23%) via his researches and invention of a new gravity formula: The General Relativity Theory. Gravity might have been responsible for the aspect of the so called "dark matter": Why do planets not circulate faster around their star? They "normally should be able to do so. Some mysterious force (hidden gravity?) seems to slow down the velocity of the planets. And because this force was not visible, is was called "dark matter". After all, in the current thought patterns, primarily matter can develop a gravitational pull.

(By the way: as well black holes can develop gravitational pull (according to our findings).

But here (still) many other "mysteries" (like our space-formula) work).

Einstein did not find the (gravity) force of "dark matter". But instead, a new, more comprehensive gravitational theory, his "General Relativity Theory", with which the theories of Isaac Newton (why and how the planets circulate around their stars) are corrected: As to Einstein, planets define their orbit by themselves. This is based on their initial energy and their "space-absorbtion-force" – in close correlation to the "space-absorbtion-force" of their star. This leads to orbits within curved-space-roads, with different curvature-strengths, depending on the distance to the star and the matter and velocity of the planet. Finally, with this theory, now as well the orbit of Mercure could be reasonably be explained. An aspect, which was not possible with the formulas of Isaac Newton.

Picture: Room Absorption & Curved Space

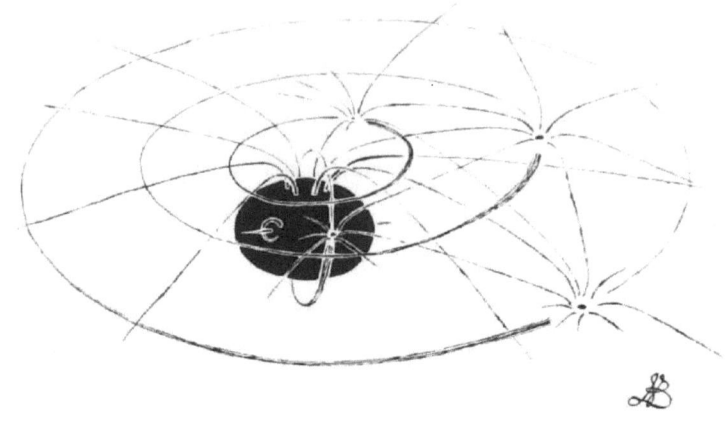

However, Einstein did not find "dark matter" with his gravitational formula. Therefore, our presumption was that the solution found by Einstein's "curved space" may not be 100% correct after all.

We simply could not believe that 5% matter should be able to influence 23% "dark matter" or 72% "dark energy". After the discovery of the space formula we considered both "dark" forces to be correlated with space. But on a different way, as Einstein defined.

But Newton's approach (the star determines the orbits of its planets with its gravity and centrifugal force) is not right either, as Mercury (pictured above, close to the sun) has a different orbit than all the other planets in the solar system.

B.8.2. Cross-correlation between energy from simpler and general relativity and gravity as well as "speed".

In my first book, "Astronomic Solutions," I started developing an economic model based on astronomy – and needed a "crisis situation". I needed a contrast to Einstein's Simple Relativity, which I had defined as the "boom situation" for various reasons.

Here I put Einstein into perspective by extrapolating Newton. I have determined the "E" via extrapolation of gravity. The same energy, which Einstein gets via "extrapolation" of matter (via c^2) in his Simply Relativity Theory. This also sounds plausible, because in super-novas and black-holes (extreme gravity) not only all matter, but also the energy (from matter) gets "lost". "Rest stars", quasars, seem to "spread" further energy into space for a long time. (Black holes, on the other hand, seem to destroy and devour everything. That's where potentially something else (Time? Space? Anti-matter? Anti-energy?) might play a role.

We now have two <u>extremes</u>: Energy resulting from multiplying matter with c^2. And energy resulting from extreme gravity, squeezing all matter-components, at the black hole.

The quantity of Energy is limited. A solution must lay between the extremes. The solution for the ("up to yesterday") unknown forces of 95% (23% dark matter, 72% dark energy) must result out of aspects already considered. It must be one or more of the dimensions with which we calculate, but which we don't understand in depth. That's why we focused on time and space – within the existing aspects. But looking and experimenting different.

We are aware that there is currently nothing faster than the speed of light. A c^2 therefore cannot exist as a speed. But those who have looked closely also see that our space and time formulas are not just about speed, but that we suspected completely different forces behind space and time. And these forces can very well tolerate the "square", which seems to be not verifiable as (only) speed.

However, "dark matter" cannot be deciphered, not even by Einstein's new gravitational formula, the General Theory of Relativity. Other forces work here.

B.8.3. Our "space waves" versus the "curved space" of Albert Einstein.

Albert Einstein's presumption that gravity also occurs in the form of "waves" has only just been verified. Also, in my approach (from "Astronomic Solutions"), the "relativization of Einstein via extrapolation of Newton's gravity", I was able to verify Einstein's guess: $G = E$.

With our formula, where space as well may be extrapolated, we show that space in the extreme – as well as gravity in the extreme – can be "energy". Thus, a kind of energy-

"waves" can be assumed. These waves have different properties:

1.) In low concentration, space waves provide 3-dimensional space: the space we know. This phenomenon is/was essential ...

... at the big bang. Space was needed for the big bang to occur at all;

... for the positioning of the planets in relation to their star: There, where (among others) the respective space-waves (from the star and from the planet) are similar, there will be the orbit of the planet

   a. I hereby claim, that the space-"absorption" force introduced by Einstein is more like a "displace-ment" force – and is caused by the "time" variable:
   Although…

      i. concerning "matter"
      time and gravity are in posi-tive correlation (together

they become stronger or weaker) - as opposed to …

ii. concerning "space"

their forces act in the opposite direction: time displaces space, while gravity would like to absorb all, as well space.

(space and time, tend to be in a contradiction correla- tion – when one variable grows, the value of the other decreases);

iii. In star/planet proximity, time is more concentrated – and space waves are displaced

iv. The further away from the star/planet, the more the wave concentration of space increases – and time-waves decrease.

v. The contradiction of time- and gravity-forces lead to a double effect of forces for the black-hole:

1. on the one hand, gravity absorbs all in its surrounding, and ..
2. on the other hand, time displaces space. And with the space being displaced, no force, no space-waves, which are needed for the positioning of the orbits of the planets, are there any longer
3. This explain the "mystery" of that tremendous power of the black hole ... ☺

2.) In high concentration - far away from the gravity of planets/stars or black holes - space transforms into (ever narrower and more concentrated) "energy waves". Close to extreme gravitation, space-concentration tends to nothingness. Features that can confirm this are: ...

... the extrapolated formula of space proves this mathematically

... Light (electromagnetic photon waves) "tends" to space – more concentrated farer away from the stars

    a. When light from a <u>distant</u> star passes near to another, <u>closer</u> star, between us and the distant star, it is deflected outwards

        i. We are convinced that this is <u>not</u> due to the "space curvature" that Einstein suspected ...

        ii. we are convinced that this is done by a greater space-(wave) concentration (more space), the further away you are from a star/planet.

        - Light does not necessarily go the direct way, not even as a laser light. If there are further holes in the partition, directly next to the direct path of the laser beam through a hole in a partition wall, then the light also tries to get through the side-holes in order to reach the target faster overall. Although light by today's definition "has no mass," the photon-quantums still follow mass-particle laws – and take every opportunity to optimize their path to be faster.

- Light will thus also choose the path where there is more space besides this star or planet in a constellation where a star "stands in the way": when passing the star/planet, light gets space (in greater concentration) farer away from the star/planet, that it is passing by. So, light first turns away from the star, and then follows the "normal-space ratios" again (once the "disturbing" planet/star is gone). Then no distraction occurs anymore.

- On planets/stars, the time concentration is greater than the space concentration. Since time – as opposed to gravity – is displacing space, light will turn away from a star, when passing by. On the other side, light is attracted and even may be swallowed by the gravity of extreme powerful black holes. How can this be?:

a) At stars the matter is strong. Therefore, time is strong as well. Strong enough, to displace space against the gravity power tendency.

b) At "medium-power" black holes, there is still matter in the surroundings. Weak matter, as it will be destroyed soon. Weak matter leads to weak time. Still, light may pass this medium-strong-black-hole, as some space-waves will still be around in the neighborhood.

c) at strong black-holes matter (becomes zero) is being destroyed far away from the center. Space collapses to nothing (E/0 is not defined, is nothing). Light has no space to circuit around. Time is dead (0/x remains zero). The force of big gravity gains and destroys all. As well light.

Space consists of weaker or stronger waves-concentrations – but is not curved ... 😊 .

b. The "space curvature" is therefore "only" a stronger space-energy-wave concentration, which attracts the energetic light to itself, because it can fly faster here.

c. The planet-"space-absorption" of Einstein is therefore rather a "time-force-concentration" on the star/planet, which pushes the light away, towards space.

3.) The combination of time and space is the aspect which seems to determine the distance of the planets to the star. The formulas of space and time contain matter and energy. And in the time and space combination also the energy of speed is included – which Einstein used for his space-absorbing power. But now that we have the formulas of space and time, we can argue more specific.

B.8.4. Oval Orbits

Planets optimize their orbits to keep their dwell and range along the star as short as possible, as Einstein found out. We suspect, probably also in order not to get into the catches of the gravitational pull of the star and to avoid getting stuck on it. A circular orbit would actually suffice, but there is precisely this tendency towards the oval.

The oval course shortens the time at the star. And: the oval allows for an even longer and deeper stay in the areas of more concentrated space, further away from the star – and thus a disproportionate gain in "freedom" instead of "bounded" by gravity.

Just like the light, or the total universe, as well planets seem to aspire more space, higher space concentrations. Space is an energy that represents a counter-force to gravity. ☺

B.8.5. The solution to the mysterious "dark matter".

In high concentration, space-energy waves are the long-sought "dark matter". "Dark matter" is a fallacy, because one did not know the formulas of time and space.

"Dark matter" is a force that supposedly causes gravity, slowing down the planets velocity by their star, for example. But this force is bigger than the star is able to provide, as stars have correspondingly to little matter/mass for that dimension of breaking. A mystery - until now ... because...

a. the planets fly as fast as they should – we just don't see it because we can't see energy waves (except light).
b. the density of space (waves) increases the further away you are from the star.
    i. The most distant stars would have to suffer most visually error from the assumed "dark matter" if our theory is correct. They should actually be much "faster" than the planets more closer to the star.
c. we measure our speed in space (km) per hour (h). However, when space (km) is concentrated, every km is shorter, more concentrated – and the speed becomes faster (not visible to us), because the planet maintains its speed despite the shorter space-wave distance.

With this approach, we solve 23% of the previously 95% of unknown energy. The energy from the "dark matter", which we now fill with space-energy-wave concentrations.

It is interesting that both, the universe as such strives for growth (space-energy waves) and the light strives for space (further holes in the partition or higher space concentrations further away from stars/planets). And even the planets in a galaxy aspire to space, away from their star. Free space in its energetic-form, freedom, is a status, that is also aspired in universe.

But the space in its 3-D form is also needed: free space to be able to act, to work.

And the combination of energetic and 3-D space is also pursued: freedom. Freedom of thought (energy) and action (planet: orbit optimization, light: hole search in wall) is sought by both the universe and humans. Lamentably this is not always possible and not everywhere. There would be more prosperity if it were the way as in the universe: everyone searches, develops and optimizes its own "path (space) through life". The financial basis for this (based on astronomical aspects) was presented in the first book, AstronTimeOnomy.

What is interesting about the extrapolation of our space formula is that space does not primarily have the 3-D orientation. The universe is not (mainly) about regional expansion. We are now certain that the universe, with its "expansion", is more likely to strive for the energetic state of space.

The territorial power-expansion efforts of rulers were and are not useful for the well-being of humanity and nature.

In order to achieve greater prosperity on Earth, energy-"space" should be promoted. In our opinion, this comparable kind of energetic-space lies primarily in people's minds, in people's brains – and is more than just knowledge. Most of the energy comes from wisdom, which is based on knowledge.

The only raw material on earth, which increases in use, is **knowledge or wisdom (space-energy universal counterpart).** Knowledge is thus comparable to the aspect observed in space of achieving (free)"space" by converting matter into energy. We should also strive for ideas and know-how rather than primarily material things. Then there would be more peace liberty, welfare and sustainability on earth.

The only status on earth, which can keep up with the dimensions for atoms (at the outside "border" of the universe), is **Freedom (space, as universal counterpart).** And the freedom we mean, is more than purely formalist freedom. In particular, it is the freedom of thought – and the social tolerance and acceptance of thoughts – even if they have not been verified by current "knowledge status-quo-institutions" like universities. Wisdom cannot be institutionalized. On the contrary, the more institutionalized, the less creativity will be possible*[7]. Wisdom arises primarily where freedom prevails – not formalism, dirigisme, centralism (no gravity).

The best pack, which represents the coexistence of the systems for a common goal (free-space extraction – each optimizes its own path – and coordinates with the others via gravitational waves and space-time waves), is peace (energy as universal counterpart). And peace can only come about with widespread and valid (as well mental) freedom.

The best remedy to enable each person to find their own way - while respecting the goals of the whole - is the granting of the LAZEB ("Lebens-Arbeits-Zeit-Einheiten-Bonus", life-working-time-unit bonus – in line with the start-energy that each star gets for its entire life at its time of creation). On the basis of TV (Time-Value) as a time currency. With LAZEB, there is a chance of transcendence (the highest level of the Maslow Pyramid of Needs) for every human being. Thus, a great commitment to the well-being of this world as a whole will arise. Just as the universe strives for the well-being of all its participants through space-energy generation.

C. Spacial Aspects on Earth – In search of a better economy, sociology and peace and liberty model.

Through its "space" expansion and extrapolated transformation of "space" into energy, the universe manages to have very few major crises (1–2 supernovas every 100 years). The management of the "intelligent" people on earth is not as successful (99% of all companies founded 100 years ago collapse due to various crises).

C.1. Territorial & monarchy-oriented developments – hardly human rights at all

Egyptians, Chinees, Greeks, Italians, Romans, Arabs, Spaniards, Portuguese, French, Dutch, Danes, English, Germans, Russians, Americans, Turks, Koreans, ...

A lot of nations have had their experience with the delusion of power, and especially territorial megalomania, of monarchs or (quasi-)dictators. In such constellations there are always a ruler, a strong hierarchy – and very many right- and middle-less people, who have to serve as slaves and soldiers for the power, territory and wealth aspirations of the rulers.

But too large areas (matter) without enough power (energy) disintegrate (implode, like a super-nova in space). The former power is falling apart because of its megalomania is difficult to handle. And because of many people who at some point no longer want to be dictated. Who want to go their own way.

In parallel with the continuously disintegrating monarchies/ dictatorships, more affluent craftsmen, merchants and more and more specialists developed, who secured more and more rights. In the end, however, this development also faces the dilemma that once again only individual overpowering capital owners can no longer sell the goods and services they offer, because the rest of the population, as well as states, are impoverished. The capital system has therefore already imploded several times – and threatens to implode again.

C.2. Material/ capital-oriented developments – human rights only in the case of prosperity

C.2.1. Agricultural economy

The old agricultural economy needed land, a lot of land, to harvest grain and to let cattle graze. At that time, land was the guarantor of prosperity. That is another reason why there were many wars to win land.

Today, agriculture can be practiced on a minimal area in greenhouses – and the plants can be faked for three days in just one day using artificial light to achieve faster growth. Together with an efficient water supply, this leads to drastic crop increases. Land is no longer so interesting militarily. At least not for intelligent politicians*8.

Capital has dramatically optimized agriculture. And as well provided a better and healthier diet for the world's population. In the age of overproduction, however, these advances are partly destroyed by the law of profitability. Some of the overproduction is being destroyed even though there is hunger in the world. Or it is offered at dumping prices on the world markets, at which even developing countries - with far lower wages - cannot compete with. Overproduction and subsidies are destroying infrastructure in developing countries that originally were able to produce these goods - and mostly cheaper. If the people of these areas were wealthy and knowing (energetic space), they would not buy the cheaper, often subsidized goods from abroad. But they would produce them by themselves.

C.2.2. Industrial economy

What was already hinted at in agriculture (becoming settled, 3-field economy, greenhouses): the concentration in little space, developed extremely further in the Industrial Revolution. Many locations, where huge specialized. Industries for special products were created. And the specialization went deep, until the last single step in production. Space (as a surface) was hardly needed any more. (The energetic form of) space (in the brains) had (and has) far more value.

Capital has increased prosperity in developed countries through mass production and favorable prices – but mostly to the detriment of developing countries.

The low prices for technology and comfort have led to an extreme material and individualistic orientation. The well-being of humanity, nature and the environment has been ignored.

Space crystalized (materialized) into stately apartments and houses, top cars, PCs, mobile phones, etc. But a lot of energy has also been invested in education – at least in the developed world. The general dissemination of knowledge has contributed far more to prosperity than the respective optimizations of machines. Lamentably, the last mentioned is now destroying not only the wealth of developing countries with low prices of (partly subsidized) developments and mass-overproductions. But machine-automatization is destroying the wealth as well in developed countries, as workers are not needed any more. And by replacing workers by machines capital is killing itself:

there will be no buyers anymore if no one gets any salary anymore. That is one of the vicious circles within our actual capital systems.

C.2.3. Service Economy

The service economy only needs space, if at all, as a logistics, transport or (off)delivery or (virtual) service location. The service as such can be done at a minimal point anywhere in the world. Space as a land gain is no longer needed.

Investment capital is far less needed in the services sector than in the industrial economy. Much more skill and knowledge (spiritual space) is needed – and much greater specialization is needed to achieve effective gains here as well.

The material focus of the industrial age is accompanied or replaced by a wave of immaterial life reliefs and pleasures. Cars need to be cheaper to compete with the money spent on holidays. And cars are no longer purchased in big quantities, but carsharing-services are replacing the "one car for each person" strategy of the past.

C.2.4. Automated Economy

Investment capital needs to automate more and more – and make everything more and more affordable. People are replaced by machines and computers (Industry 4.0), which work in convenient locations, 365 days p.a., 24 hrs./day, without vacation or illness. Unit costs by machine fall below the manufacturing costs by labor - even of those from developing countries.

In the Internet world, you don't even have to concentrate the few remaining workers in a location (somewhere in the world), but you can assemble know-how from the apartments/work-rooms of specialists from all over the world. Space (as an area) becomes waste – at least for the provision of services.

For the provision of services, however, from agriculture to the automatic economy, another space has become more and more important: the mental space, the electronics in our brains. This development is extremely important for the next great wave of development after the monarchy and capital epochs: the individual economy (see below).

For the final phase of capital concentrations, specialists with high intelligence are of course also required to develop artificial intelligence (further). In the final phase of capital concentration, however, hardly any people are needed for the production of goods or the execution of services any more. Everything is done via computers and machines.

Capital has automated everything. And sawn off his own branch. After all, what should people consume when they are all unemployed and poor? And without wage taxation, the state is also bankrupt, because taxing capital is hardly possible - as it is very fluctuating.

But the 1% of humanity that now owns all the capital, cannot consume as much as the 99% who are now unemployed. New models are required.

C.2.5. Problems and contradictions of capital models

To develop new things, it is good to discover the mistakes of the old. Thinking outside the box, cross-thinking and looking at things from a bird's eye view is always good. Creativity is even more effective if you have an ideal, a vision, a dream, a model in which everything works better (in our case: the universe). You may achieve better results through comparisons and solution-search. With a universe perspective, we see the following challenges in the capital and material-focused society of the earthly mankind.

In the first book, AstronTimeOnomy, we transferred the astronomical dimension of TIME to Earth and to its models (time is money? OK: Money, be time!). And as well the idea of a big bonus at birth. Like the stars get their energy for their life-time, when they arise.

In this actual book, we transfer the dimension of SPACE into our GlobalOnomy model: What can be done when demand, supply and capital aspects change so dramatically, as in the past decades?

C.2.5.1. Demand is a function of capital ...

... but capital needs demand to act.

A cycle that is difficult to start going. From an astronomical point of view this already gives rise to a presumption, which will later be consolidated by further in-coherences: This process can only be initiated with an "external energy". And will just be adding up to zero change in wealth, if all would be calculated the right way. And this energy would then be missing somewhere else. And needs to be "paid back" somewhere else. In the end, when you add everything and subtract negative late sequences (like pollution), it tends to be a zero-sum game, if not mental breakthroughs optimize many aspects – as a new kind of "new initial energy".

Einstein's relativity equations represent the now. With the formulas of space and time, we found new multiplicators, that un-cover the up to now hidden 95% of "dark" forces. The biggest multiplicator for wealth does not lie in understanding the present. Nor does it lie in the (finally:) zero-sum game of un-equal take (too much) and give (too-little) – because that is no astronomy-conform equation. The last is an earth / mankind-made inequation, that time and again leads to implosions. The multiplicator for wealth lies in knowledge and wisdom, in creative break-throughs. And that is more than the multiplying factor of Einstein´s "c^2" towards our "m" matter-optimization by productivity increasing aspects. This secret multiplicator is our amplification of that "c^2"-multiplicator - with time and space. And if we now implement our time and space ideas on earth, that would be that kind of "initial energy" needed, to get the world towards universe efficiency and wealth.

The demand that capital needs for its products must be created by or with capital. This can be done via e.g.: paying wages, but this means a lengthy process in which many other capital-investing companies must also be active. It is easier to attract states to the capital model, which generate demand-tuning through ever-increasing debt and credit bubbles, money or/and social benefits or/and infrastructure or/and raw material mining approvals, etc. Later, capital has to fight for its own products demand over competitive displacement. To do so, it has to exploit areas with little "voting rights", such as the "environment" (damages) or/and the third world, to keep cheaply and destructively, to achieve (mainly) own success.

After innovation implementations, the process optimizations usually only serve to crowd out competition in order to become stronger themselves.

The eye of the needle is also, that there always is too little demand and/or money/capital.

And with general demand reductions (crises), the state helps with subsidies, bad banks, money printing, etc. But this is just a "bond" for the future.

And if at some point this cycle collapses due to a lack of credibility in terms of back-payment ability, then once again a capital model (another bubble) is broken. As long as it is "only" about capital, this is not threatening too much – although much enough. But when it comes to the environment and our fellow human beings, it is about our lives. And then many capital models are suboptimal.

In our first book, AstronTimeOnomy, we have therefore built a model that solves the demand problem. However, capital can no longer act at will. For wealthy and intelligent people around the world, capital must act sustainably. Mass production is then rather the exception, since then there are many wealthy individualists and (according to Maslow) probably also much more transcendent and less profiling neurotic, since everybody is wealthy. This would also reduce the primarily material orientation of our today's industrial society. In favor of other, rather mental orientations and profiling. It would be nice if the space-energy-dimension of our brains no longer thinks old-fashioned: "I buy things that I don't need – with money that I don't have – to impress people that I don't like." It would be nice if there were more empathy and sustainability.

More knowledge and wisdom space for a better mankind and environment.

C.2.5.2. Capital must concentrate – i.e. itself become larger – against the others..

... but by concentrating, it destroys its potential demand – and thus itself.

Once a capital model is implemented, it needs to grow larger. It doesn't matter what model it is: real estate funds, auto-credit funds, venture capital-financed start-ups, cars, banks, bad-banks, "what-ever-it-takes" state-, bank-&-company debt, bubbles, tax models, subsidy models, industrial states (vs. all other states) ... . All models want more and more and need to get bigger and bigger. Also, at the expense of all other "important" areas. Because in the end the only one thing that counts politically is: "too big, to fail". The "too big" gains further support from the state. All other "important!" areas collapse. The sad thing is, that a lot of people promote this process of self-destruction by speculating and hoping to make profits from "nothing."

However, if capital can no longer live off interest because demand at / for the investment-sectors products is falling. And if investments in the interest-rate capital market are not worthwhile. Then (that too much) capital must speculate. States themselves are to blame for many faults through their zero-interest-rate policies. And, also because more and more bubbles are forming to maintain the semblance of growth, of size, via extremely growing bubbles.

Speculation, however, is a "zero-sum game" par excellence. 1 side gains, 1 side loses. At each share that is sold or purchased. In sum, however, there is no wealth gain – or only for very few. Because only those who know more or have more influence, will win. And the one who wins can stand out – but only briefly. Because if the world loses all its money towards top speculators, then there is no money left for demand. And without demand, capital is sawing at its own branch. A rather "remarkable" model – at least in the long term and concerning sustainably. Lamentably states are (in)directly involved. They are themselves so indebted that they partly speculated in the hope, to get out of the vicious circle of credits and bubbles, which they could no longer finance (see HRE, West-LB, HSH-Nordbank, LBBW, ...). And as well participations in companies through which profits could (indirectly) be made with speculation make some "sense" for states. In the car-industry the state has a stake of up to 30%, the post and lottery are statal, and as well railways and roads are of the state, etc.. Therefore, it will be difficult to prohibit speculation.

But speculation would be one of the first suboptimal projects to be eliminated on Earth to lure money primarily into more efficient projects. That kind of projects that increase real(!) productivity through intelligence. Projects, that achieve more, than just a zero-sum game. Zero-sum-games, which in the end – in the absence of demand – even saws at their own branch. Sadly, how much political incompetence still continues to support this kind of models*8. Nevertheless: Hope dies last.

C.2.5.3. Capital must increase profitability

... and ultimately destroys itself through the compulsion to automate.

Jobs. They are being destroyed by the pressure for profitability, even those in developing countries. Once invested, capital does not always become more profitable. (In)direct competing products can destroy the investments made. Continued increases in profitability and price reductions reduce the temptation of competitors to invest in competing products.

When capital was still expensive or/and scarce – and there were too few inventions for further automation – workers had to be hired to produce and grow more.

Capital is being "produced" in tremendous amounts. But the states have accumulated too much debt. That might have had increase interest rates despite the money amount. Thus, together(!) with all(!) central banks they decided to cut interest rates. Down to a "fixed" low level. This maintains debt servicing more "favorable". Without having to make too many cuts to budgets. And since official capital at this mini-interest rate could not be obtained from the market, it was decided to print even more money. In "what-ever-it-takes" dimensions. To preserve states and banks from going bankrupt. Nevertheless, states, banks, insurance companies, ailing companies, etc. had to be helped with many trillions to cure one wound after another. And since many banks still cannot give credits, large companies are allowed to obtain direct loans from the ECB.

Capital has become abundant and cheap. Rationalization ideas up to artificial intelligence have become more. And work is becoming more and more expensive – in developed countries. Of course, automation, the replacement of jobs by machines and computers, is the actually best way to increase profitability. Especially, as at the time, manual manufacturing costs in troubled developing countries have become cheaper. And additionally, unemployed people get at maximum a lower social payment – and therefore only buy cheap as well. Capital must adapt. Continuously.

A vicious circle that is costing more and more jobs, including in developing countries. But it also reduces global demand, due to a lack of higher wages. However, this means that the productive-investment-sector is lacking of demand. Previous Investment-capital now fluctuates to speculative-capital. Too much speculative bubbles are being built up now by too much capital. Until everything implodes.

States. Wage sums are falling. If there are fewer jobs – and no alternatives develop – then payrolls are missing. They are missing for consumption as demand and as fiscal-basis on consumption and production. And they are missing as a fiscal basis on earnings and wages, for the states. These funds are lacking at the states for their investments, maintenance and all social transfers. There is a lack of money for unemployment-payments, as well as for new minimum-wage-guarantee-models that might maintain social peace (the latter could anyway only be afforded by rich states, if redistributed). Without payrolls, states also implode – according to the capital laws in force today.

Nature. Nature must also be exploited cheapest, if capital profitability falls, due to lack of demand, lower wages of consumers, fewer recipients of benefits, etc. Capital must become more profitable all the time, otherwise it will go bankrupt, which could lead to even worse damage.

C.2.5.4. Capital must fluctuate ...

... and leaves behind "burnt earth", which is also difficult to use for alternatives.

States that can't (no longer) or do no longer want to keep up with capital-requirements, go out empty-handed. When in the "own" country the prospects are low and interest rates are high, capital flows abroad. Projects are built on this basis. But when capital (again) has better prospects elsewhere, the projects stop. And there will be not much left except debt. No capital, not even for own ways, because the capital rules do not allow new or more debt.

When investment capital is faced with a decline in demand, it must fluctuate into speculative capital in order to continue to generate profits. In the absence of alternatives, speculative bubbles are built up with many tricks. The "insiders"-capital leaves these bubbles before they implode. The losers are mostly the late entrants and retail investors, as well as states, trying to avoid more damage by subsidizing the bubble-problems. They remain stuck on losses – which again lead to generally declining demand – and lead to the move of capital into other models. Quite often, just new bubbles.

In the final phase of fluctuation, before a currency devaluation, tangible assets become interesting again. Gold, silver, diamonds and works of art are then becoming interesting and more and more expensive. And therefore, also bought as a lucrative speculative and alternative security-aspect. But then, the same results come up again and again: money devaluations and (in-)direct expropriations, such as forced, imposed mortgages on home ownership.

After all the burned earths, the remaining capital would then be at an end as well, with no value at all. If all the damage was added together, there would not be much left of the wealth of capital. Especially if there is a war for the preservation of "national" interest, as has been happening so often, repeatedly.

C.2.5.5. The competition against itself ...

... capital is its own – and greatest adversary.

While the "normal" people of all nationalities can live well together, in many "power centers" of this world it unfortunately looks very sad. Life frustration, hatred and the pursuit of power always destroy a lot of prosperity. Worse is the incompetence in some of these power centers. And the rage of destruction, at whatever cost – to impose one's own wishes. Even in civilized states.

However, quantity- & concentration-growth-urge & -coercion always ends in a too great "size" for the respective "leaders". As with the monarchies or with too big stars, the system will collapse: like a "super-nova" in astronomy. Inevitably, over and over again. It's a system error.

The laws of capital are like cancer in an initially healthy body, or like a too big growing star. What becomes too big and has too little "energy" (aspects like: death of dictator and/or competence or/and followers or/and controlling-mechanisms or/and capital, etc.) to be able to continue to grow, in order to be able to continue to circulate in the "space" with enough energy, destroys itself. The laws of the universe also apply on Earth.

At the moment, everyone is once again hoping, that better times will come, to stabilize everything again. Unfortunately, we haven't seen a model, which would be able to do so. Except for our GlobalOnomy-model, which we started to explain in the books AstronTimeOnomy and AstronSpaceOnomy.

It is time for a new time. A time, in which also space (openness) for new(!) space (theoretical models) exists. In this book, AstronSpaceOnomy, we have looked at this time and again. Now we want to look at it a little bit more concrete.

C.3. The individual society - global human & environmental rights

"Prosperity" is not considered in any constitution as a "fundamental right". Not even in Germany, where Ludwig Erhardt had the chance to implement it, being one of the latest constitutions. "Monetary stability", a fundamental aspect for the value-preservation of prosperity is not a fundamental right in any constitution either.

So, neither the capital-rules (as seen before) nor the constitutions seem to focus on wealth nor welfare for their inhabitants. While the church promotes poverty openly – states keep their doors open for anti-welfare & -wealth decisions. It looks like there is a consensus in the aspect, that "poor people are easier to handle". If you are in need of money, you will obey.

Most citizens, as well in industrialized countries, lamentably are puppets of politicians. Working at least 50% of the years time just for the taxes, gets people quite poor in comparison to what they could do with all the money they have to pay to the state.

And lamentably, there is no big choice for us puppets. Just every 4 years an election out of about 5 "main" prefabricated and quite similar programs, is not really a big choice.

We want to change that. With the laws of astronomy to improve economy & currency, knowledge & wisdom, peace & liberty, health & wealth, and welfare & sustainability.

We have presented a better wealth model with monetary stability in the first book, AstronTimeOnomy. In the current book, AstronSpaceOnomy, the main focus lays on the aspects of peace and liberty – being "associated" with "free space" of universe

C.3.1. World wide wealth - in peace and liberty: AstronTimeOnomy- and AstronSpaceOnomy- aspects.

There used to be two professions: hunters and gatherers. Both were always needed.

Today, there are more than 100,000 occupations in categorization lists. Specializations would break any list. However, the individual skills are often only used in individual companies and here often only temporarily. They are definitely needed, but it does not pay for companies to hire these specialists as employees. Highly professional people have to do other secondary activities in order to survive until they find a return to their specialty. A waste of resources and opportunities for prosperity.

For each individual person, LAZEB (the LifeWorkTimeUnitsBonus) *[11] is an immense freedom to shape its life. And to offer his know-how and work where it is needed. While staying where you feel comfortable. Brilliant conditions. Like in the universe, where a) every star gets its life-time-energy when arising and b) space for each participant planet/star is constantly growing.

And that every human being will seek specialization and his own way in space is in the nature of things. Einstein found that each planet seeks and optimizes its own path. Parents need to quickly realize that their babies are initially crawling only small circles around them. But these circles are getting bigger and bigger - until they have to run after the children ...

Of course, education requires a certain channeling – also in order to be able to determine where the interests of the respective child lie. But this channeling should be as open as possible to allow free space for realizing real preferences, desires, and ideas, with which these new people can generate new growth and prosperity.

We need a re-orientation. Away from primarily materialistic mass-consumption behavior. And towards taking into account more individual preferences. This is also made possible by more freedom and LAZEB. If everyone has a secure existence, there is more chance, that one can continue to educate oneself, achieve wisdom, as well as think and act transcendently. And thus, we will be able to take more care of one's fellow human beings and the environment.

The basis of SPACE (FREE ROOM) and TIME (LAZEB, TV) can help to solve the challenges of the upcoming developments and vicious circles and all those exploding bubbles of our capital models:

1.) Demand is a function of capital -
   But: Capital needs demand to act
      i. This vicious circle can be solved with LAZEB. In the universe, each star gets the energy for its entire life when it arises in the universe. Out of the "nothing". The ECB has proved that money as well can be printed out of "nothing" in "What-Ever-It-Takes"-amounts. So why not solve the perpetual demand problem with

LAZEB (LifeWorkingTime-UnitsBonus). But not as a salary from the state. There are no sustainability, too much different interests and a too big danger of money getting lost by mismanagement, as the past has shown time and again. And would only be possible within rich states. And a (low) salary would keep people poor and dependent. A bonus, at an independent institution, not based on the actual nothingness, but on the basis of future action (life-work), would solve many current problems (see book: AstronTimeOnomy)

2.) Capital must always become more profitable – and automate (acute Industry 4.0 problem)

But: Without jobs: no salary, no taxes, no social benefits - and no demand ... Ultimately, capital destroys itself with its laws

   a. This vicious circle can be solved with LAZEB. See above.

3.) Capital must concentrate – and destroy competition (be cheaper than 3rd world wages)
But: Only 1 (remaining) rich man can't consume as much as 7 billion people...

Ultimately, capital destroys itself with its own laws:

   i. With LAZEB, all people become individualists and transcendent.   Mass production   is   not worthwhile, because no "rich" wants to have a mass product. Individuality is also most likely to be performed locally   (culturally conditioned).   Ideational,

SPACE, is more important
than products, MATTER.

4.) Time is money? OK: Money, be time! :
TV (time valuta), the new currency
system(see AstronTimeOnomy) is built
on astronomy thoughts about SPACE
and TIME. And it is many times more
stable than the current insane money-
quantity production, zero-interest-rate-
imposed politically, bad-banks,
phantom-companies, speculative-
bubbles and debt-records, all of which
pass only fake sustainability tests.
The universe has been proving us
sustainability for 13.8 billion years. Why
not adopt many of its aspects? These
sustainability aspects and their transfer
opportunities will be discussed in the
next book, AstronEfficiencyOnomy.

5.) There will continue to be mass
productions, but on a different,
especially more sustainable, basis.
Demand for these mass-products will
not go away, as now all mankind may

be buying whatever needed (through general LAZEB wealth). But mass-product-consumption per individual household will fall, compared to the new income and new preferences.

6.) The much-evoked empathy, needed to absorb all the unemployment challenges created by the stark developments of Industry 4.0 has a financing base with LAZEB. The empathetic commitment (SPACE) can now be used to offer his fellow human beings new perspectives, to identify and guide one's own preferences and abilities, to go own ways, to create ones´ own (life), in ones´ own SPACE.

7.) With LAZEB and the feasibility of own paths, no one needs to become a soldier out of sheer need for money. No rich man goes to war. And with the existential LAZEB, the jungle-tree-feller can now turn to become jungle-forester.

C.3.2. Co-steering - swiveling liberty

The results of the French Revolution Liberté, Égalité, Fraternité were great. But the people have very easily allowed these achievements to be taken back by new rulers. Because they have not been involved any more in debates. If politicians and/or makers can do what they want, they do. Power-addicted people must be challenged and channeled by a wealthy, awake, intelligent and wise people. Not the desires of those greedy for power, but the really best for everyone and everything must be pursued. The state should be kept to a minimum. The freedom (and real wealth) of each individual must be one of the highest goals. The SPACE aspects of the universe show us the right way!

Freedom, peace and sustainability in prosperity are values to which we will devote at www.Wise-Star.org (still under "construction"). We would be very pleased to welcome you on this platform as a member or/and sponsor, as well as, of course on the actual platform, www.world-wide-wealth.com

The customer is king? OK: "Kings," become "customers" !!!

Purely rhetorically, one is "king". De facto, however, we only are the "must!-consumer" of the produced mass-products.

In order to optimize the world, it is possible to start now. Just challenge! Check sustainability for the things you buy. Be yourself – individualists instead of someone else from advertising or politics with whom you are supposed to identify. Go your own way. If you don't go your way, sooner or later you'd be gone anyway. And you're not wasting time now.

Collaborate with us to implement a new system. Become a member of world-wide-wealth.com (or in future Wise-Star.org) or become politically or socially active. Somewhere. For your interest. So that those who want to deprive you of your freedom, your space, cannot do it as they like. The world needs guarding, awake people. Only in this way the necessary vitality, the energy of the universe, will arise. Life does not mean vegetating around and only making your rounds in the hamster wheel. Life means being active, becoming aware of what you want – and striving for it.

With the LAZEB from AstronTimeOnomy, every human being is as wealthy a king. Everyone can start with the ideas of AstronSpaceOnomy, to develop and pursue their own ideas, to fulfill their own path, in their (knowledge) field.

Everyone becomes king in his activity area. And everyone becomes a strong demander. With LAZEB, there is a huge new wave of demand. What is emerging is what capital lacks today: demand. And it re-emerges with each birth. With fixed prices in function of production-costs, as well as "tolerated" profit margins. There also is no inflation – especially not, because of the reduction of the LAZEB at death. Most people then have a good education. The mental "space" will be vitally used. People are sustainable and transcendent. They know exactly what is good for them, the society and the environment.

Our vision is a global sustainable prosperity in freedom and peace. Our mission is to invent and optimize correlations in or out of the rules of astronomy. For implementation in - and optimization of - our world. Our strategy is, among other things, the summaries in books. And the gradual conviction of fellow citizens and decision-makers that our world absolutely needs a better way, a better system. We would be very pleased to receive your support. Thanks in advance.

D. Index

*1 Lee Smolin, Book: "In the Universe of Time," 2015, p. 239

*2 Wikipedia, "dark energy" and "dark matter", illustration, see a note here in the book, ANNEX 1

*3 Stephen Hawking, book: "A Briefer History of Time", 2008, p. 5

*4 Albert Bright, book: "AstronTimeOnomy", 2021, p. 27ff.

*5 Stephen Hawking, book: "A Briefer History of Time", 2008, "the twins paradox" p. 47ff.

*6 Stephen Hawking, book: "A Briefer History of Time", 2008, p. 48, 2nd passage

*7 Thomas Gainsborough "I wish you would recollect, that painting and punctuality mix like oil and vinegar, and that genius and regularity are utter enemies."

*8 Johann Gottfried: You can rule with power. Governance involves intelligence. That is why so many politicians aspire to a role as ruler.

*9 Paperback of Physics, Horst Kuchling, HANSER-Verlag, 21. Edition, 2014, p. 121f.

*10 Stephen Hawking, book "A Briefer History of Time"

*11 Albert Bright, book: "AstronZeitOnomie", 2017

*12 Albert Bright, Book: AstronManagOnomy, 2016, S31ff

*13 Stephen Hawking, "A Briefer History of Time", 2008, p. 48.

*14 Isaac Newton: G + F = 1

E. Short Description

Peace in freedom, prosperity and sustainability are very high goals. Especially because in human history they were often not really conscious or difficult to achive, and then, often disappeared all the faster.

In the universe, SPACE (free space for all "participants") is a central goal. And universe achieves it very successfully. Since 13.8 billion years. It grows and grows and grows ... - ever further, faster and for the benefit of all involved. Because with "(free) space" every planet and star can really go its own way. And if all are "spatial" (and energetic) far enough apart from each other, peace is virtually pre-programmed. The risk of collision is eliminated.

Our current industrialized world is very materialistic. And Einstein's findings are also "materially" shaped: with his "special relativity" he has the energy from ... - and with his "general relativity" the gravity of ... (visible) matter. (Visible) matter, however, only represents (0.4%) 4.6% of universal "energy".

The successful universe does not focus on matter! It focuses on "forces"! The largest are "dark matter" (23% of all energy – and has not much to do with real "matter") and "dark energy" (72% of all energy). Dark matter is deciphered in this book – and used for earthly purposes.

In "**AstronTimeOnomy**" the "value of time" has been redefined for the benefit of prosperity.

In the current book, "**AstronSpace-Onomy**", "values of space" are redefined for the benefit of freedom and peace.

" Time" and "space" are more important than "matter".

The universe promotes both. It becomes "time" for humanity to internalize this "knowledge- and wisdom- space-expansion" – and no longer primarily to act materialistically. This would make humans just as successful as the universe. It is time to pursue higher values than purely materialistic consumption. Because this world exists only once. And freedom, peace welfare and sustainability are much more valuable than materialistic consumption and profit.

F. The trilogy of GlobalOnomy:

In **AstronTimeOnomy** with the TIME formula invention, the "dark mysticism" around this dimension is ended. On the basis of these findings, a new monetary system and a new model of prosperity has been developed.

With **AstronSpaceOnomy** the SPACE formula invention i.a. the mysticism of "dark matter" (why do the planets not circulate around their star faster than they could?) is removed. On the basis of these findings, a better model of freedom, peace, welfare and sustainability is developed. This can also be financed by the previously developed prosperity model. And provides the needed "space" to the ideas of AstronTimeOnomy.

In **AstronEfficiencyOnomy** the SPACE-TIME-CORRELATIONs are developed - and the "dark energy" (why does the universe grow faster than theoretically possible?) is decrypted. The theory of "curved space" is also further refuted. Furthermore, an approach of a "perpetuum mobile" is presented. Based on these findings, a better sustainability and efficiency model is developed, which incorporates the insights from the wealth model and the freedom model.

World-wide-wealth is possible. With GlobalOnomy.

ANNEX 1: Graphics and info from "Wikipedia"xx

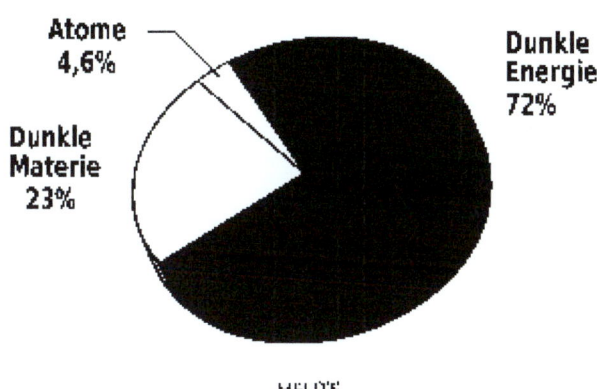

HEUTE

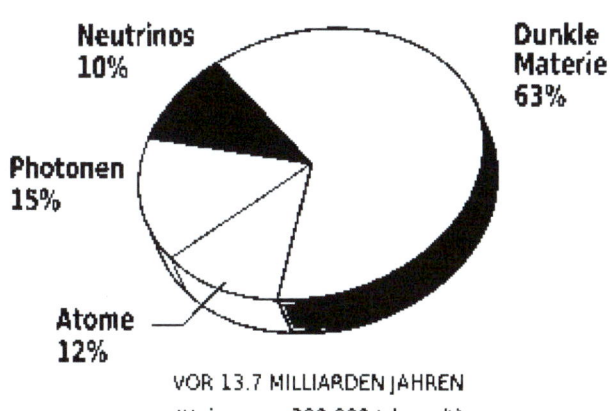

VOR 13.7 MILLIARDEN JAHREN
(Universum 380.000 Jahre alt)

135

Matter and energy portion of the universe at present (above) - and (below), 380,000 years after the big bang. (Observations of the WAMP-Mission and others.).[1] The term "atoms" stands for "normal matter".

G. SPACE for notes